BRIGHT N

CANDIDE
BY
VOLTAIRE

Intelligent Education

Nashville, Tennessee

BRIGHT NOTES: Candide
www.BrightNotes.com

No part of this publication may be used or reproduced in any manner whatsoever without written permission, except in the case of brief quotations in critical articles and reviews. For permissions, contact Influence Publishers http://www.influencepublishers.com.

ISBN: 978-1-645425-28-1 (Paperback)
ISBN: 978-1-645425-29-8 (eBook)

Published in accordance with the U.S. Copyright Office Orphan Works and Mass Digitization report of the register of copyrights, June 2015.

Originally published by Monarch Press.
Laurie Rozakis, 1981
2020 Edition published by Influence Publishers.

Interior design by Lapiz Digital Services. Cover Design by Thinkpen Designs.

Printed in the United States of America.

Library of Congress Cataloging-in-Publication Data forthcoming.
Names: Intelligent Education
Title: BRIGHT NOTES: Candide
Subject: STU004000 STUDY AIDS / Book Notes

CONTENTS

1)	Introduction to Voltaire	1
2)	Textual Analysis	
	Chapters 1 - 7	22
	Chapters 8 - 14	37
	Chapters 15 - 19	55
	Chapters 20 - 24	74
	Chapters 25 - 30	92
3)	Character Analysis	108
4)	Essay Questions and Answers	113
5)	Annotated Bibliography	119

INTRODUCTION TO VOLTAIRE

The term "Enlightenment" is often given to the intellectual quickening of the eighteenth century. As is the case with all intellectual movements of great importance and duration, it is difficult to say where, when, and how it began, and when it ended. In addition, any satisfactory definition of the Enlightenment would be so cumbersome and all-embracing as to be almost useless; any concise definition would certainly fail to take into account many thinkers and ideas of the period. Still, some generalities may be made which will prove useful.

The Enlightenment may best be considered the intellectual offspring of the scientific and philosophical movements of the seventeenth century. In turn, these movements would have been impossible were it not for the Renaissance, which saw the spirit of secular inquiry revived in Western Europe. The Reformation also made its contribution, in its destruction of what operated as a monolithic Church. This is not to say that the thinkers of the Renaissance and Reformation succeeded in viewing the world totally objectively, without dogma; rather, they aided in tearing down the medieval world view, a necessary precondition for the construction of a new one.

To these factors must be added the growth of nationalism and the rise of the middle class. Again, neither the national monarchs or the growing merchant class were necessarily scientifically oriented. They were more interested in this world than the next, however, and many of their actions and ideas supported a natural rather than a supernatural explanation of phenomena.

What did these movements and groups have in common? All stressed individualism and, by implication, reason. The Renaissance man needed to be free in order to fully exercise his faculty of reason. The religious reformer of the Reformation based a good deal of his protest on the Church's lack of individual interpretation of the Bible and its control over the secular activities of man. The nationalist stressed the uniqueness of his nation-state, as opposed to the universality of the Church. The market demanded that the merchant use reason in his dealings or be out-competed in trades that required the full use of his senses. During the Middle Ages, the intellectual stress was on the unity of man under God, the universality of the Church, the corporate nature of man (a member of a class rather than an individual in his own right), and the rewards of heaven. The stagnation of this period was shattered by the Renaissance and Reformation, by the nationalists and the middle class.

During the seventeenth century, synthesizing attempts were made to preserve some of the tenets of the old order, while admitting to the virtues of the new. After all, St. Thomas used reason in coming to his conclusions; even if the conclusions were unacceptable, his methodology was not. The scholastics of the fifteenth century believed their faith could be reasonably demonstrated, as did the scientists of the seventeenth century.

Three of the most important thinkers of the seventeenth century-and the intellectual fathers of the eighteenth century Enlightenment-were Rene Descartes (1596-1650), Sir Isaac Newton (1642-1727), and John Locke (1632-1704). Descartes attempted to create a system of philosophy by first sweeping away all preconceptions, and starting with the concept he held to be the only absolute, "I think, therefore I am." With the use of mathematics and the deductive method, Descartes went on to reconstruct the universe. God existed, he said, but only as a first mover and creator of matter and mathematical laws. "Give me extension and motion," he said, "and I will construct the universe." As a later critic remarked, "The Cartesian (follower of Descartes) attempts to explain all the phenomena of nature by matter and motion; requiring only that God should first create a sufficient quantity of each, just enough to set him at work." Thus, Descartes did away with the need for a supernatural God to explain earthly events, as well as the human soul itself.

Sir Isaac Newton built upon this philosophical foundation, attempting to formulate universal mathematical laws to explain all physical phenomena. He said, for example, that "every particle of matter in the universe attracts every other particle with a force varying inversely as the square of the distance between them and directly proportional to the product of their masses." The implication was clear; God existed-it was He who created these laws-but the universe acts in accordance with the laws, and not with His whims of the moment. Man may not be able to understand God, but he can understand these naturalistic laws. Consequently, to understand God, man must explore science and this world, and not theology and the supernatural.

Locke was an influential philosopher-his political ideas helped lay the basis for the American and French Revolutions-but his epistemological theories are what concerns us here. At birth, he said, the human mind is blank, a tabula rasa. The child receives simple ideas, which are later integrated to form complex ideas. Sensations give the mind its raw materials, and reason makes them meaningful. Thus, Locke ignores "revelation" and "spiritual truths," in his theory of knowledge. Also implicit in his philosophy is the belief that man possesses a volitional consciousness, that is, he has the capacity to choose and determine his course of action. God has given man a brain and reason, but he may use them freely.

Descartes, Newton, Locke, and their seventeenth and early eighteenth century followers provided the basis for the Enlightenment. At the same time, the student must remember that their ideas were not completely original, but based in part upon the work of the later scholastics. St. Thomas may not have agreed with any of their conclusions, but he would have recognized and accepted their methods.

THE ENLIGHTENMENT BELIEFS

The basic beliefs of the Enlightenment may be analyzed under four headings: (1) trust in reason; (2) disbelief in original sin; (3) the infallibility of scientific laws; (4) trust in the "simple" and "natural" methods and ways of life.

The thinkers of the Enlightenment believed that all knowledge was attainable through human reason. God gave man a brain and the free will to use it. If man used his mind correctly, he could comprehend the universe, and God himself. St. Augustine had said that man's function on earth was to create an earthly city as close to the City of God as possible, but contented that perfectibility was unattainable. The thinkers of the Enlightenment said that this perfect knowledge was within their grasp, and were supremely optimistic and self-confident.

The men of the Enlightenment denied the assertion, made by both Catholics and Protestants, that man was born with original sin and therefore was incapable of perfection. Instead, the Enlightenment thinkers believed that man was born without preconceptions, and was capable, through his reasoning faculty, of attaining both knowledge and virtues. The Enlightenment believed in progress, a rapid progress which took full advantage of the newly liberated human mind.

The uniform nature of the universe fascinated the men of the Enlightenment. The one who unlocked its secrets could use nature's laws to attain unlimited power. Everything was within man's grasp once the key to knowledge was discovered and used.

What was called "civilization" was, to many Enlightenment thinkers, the dead hand of the past upon the present. Institutions were encrusted with ideas and forms which may have once seemed useful, but which needed to be examined afresh, to determine whether or not any of it was meaningful. From this premise the Enlightenment men proceeded to discard most of organized religion, many concepts of the nation-state, war, economic institutions, etc. In the past, reformers had been content to patch the fabric of society; in the future, the premise went, the rotten foundations must be torn down and the task undertaken anew.

The key word of the Enlightenment, then, was reason. Through the use of reason, man would be able to uncover the natural laws set down by God, the great mathematician. If the laws were followed, then limitless progress would result. The turmoil and suffering of the world might have led others to extreme pessimism; to the man of the Enlightenment, each bit of suffering represented the opportunity to use reason to bring order, progress, and happiness to man. Thus, the Enlightenment, while deploring the present, was extremely optimistic about the future.

THE PHILOSOPHES

The ideas of the Enlightenment were spread by a group of men known collectively as the philosophes. These men were to be found in every part of the Western world: Locke and David Hume in England, Franklin and Jefferson in America, and Leibnitz and Herder in Germany, were leading thinkers of the period. But France, above all nations, was the home of the philosophes. This is what Jefferson meant when he said that every man has two countries: his own and France. Among the leading French philosophes were Montesquieu, Rousseau, Diderot, Helvetius, Turgot, Condorcet, and, of course, Voltaire.

The term, philosophes, is often misunderstood. It does not mean "philosophers" in the English sense of the term. Rather, these men were, in addition to being original thinkers, popularizers of an intellectual doctrine. All wrote complex works of philosophy, which were read widely by the intellectuals of Europe. But in addition, they wrote popular accounts, contributed to newspapers and magazines, and in other ways brought their doctrines to the other classes. Thus, we find that Rousseau's most important works were magazine essays or pamphlets; Franklin is well-known for Poor Richard's Almanac, and Jefferson's Declaration of Independence was designed to be read as a statement of political philosophy.

In this respect, the thinkers of the Enlightenment resembled those of the Renaissance. The latter group could scarcely have existed were it not for the patronage of the Church and the nobles, as well as the newly-created merchants of Europe. Contrary to popular belief, the artist of the Renaissance did not work for art's sake in a garret; instead, he more often than not was a hard-headed businessman who had the equivalent of a contract and an advance payment before beginning his work.

The Renaissance was indeed a great flowering of intellect and art, but it would have been impossible without the patronage of a select audience, who paid for the works of the period.

So it was with the Enlightenment philosophes. Like their predecessors, they catered to the upper class on occasion; the so-called "enlightened despots" were sponsors of many thinkers. Frederick the Great of Prussia liked to consider himself a philosophe. He wrote essays, poems, and plays, and invited other writers to his court. Voltaire lived for a while at Frederick's palace at Potsdam, and wrote several of his masterpieces there. Austrian Emperor Joseph II avidly read the works of the French philosophes, and attempted to reconstruct his nation on the models they gave him, often calling some of his mentors to Austria for aid and advice. The same was true, to a lesser extent, of Gustavus III of Sweden and Charles III of Spain. Catherine the Great of Russia gave lip service to the ideas of the philosophes, although in practice she was more despotic than enlightened. Still, she invited Diderot to Russia, gave bounties to Voltaire, and supported other French thinkers. She spent three years, herself, composing a set of instructions to a commission entrusted with the task of codifying Russia's laws. These instructions contain long sections drawn from Beccaria's *Crimes and Punishments* and Montesquieu's *Spirit of the Laws*.

It was in America and France, however, that the ideas of the philosophes were most widely spread. Turgot became finance minister for Louis XVI, and the French Revolution was often led and inspired by the ideas of these thinkers. During his period of rule, Robespierre attempted to remake French society according to the ideas of the Enlightenment, going so far as to create an artificial religion. Liberty, Equality, and Fraternity replaced the Christian Trinity; the carpenter's level replaced the cross as a religious symbol. The American Revolution was led by men who could be classified as philosophes. Certainly Jefferson, Franklin, Madison, Hamilton, and Washington fall into this category.

But as important as the appeal to the ruling class was it was not the substance of the philosophe's audience. Instead, the thinkers of the Enlightenment appealed to the broad and rapidly-growing middle class. One need only note the rapid growth of newspapers and magazines-typical middle class publications-in the eighteenth century to see evidence of this appeal. Whereas the men of the Renaissance appealed primarily to the thin strata of the nobility and the upper class, the philosophes wrote for the newly-articulate middle class. Diderot's seventeen-volume Encyclopedia, which included articles by Voltaire, Montesquieu, Rousseau, and almost all the major French thinkers, was written for and sold to this audience. Emotional appeals sufficed for the upper and lower classes; the upper class maintained its position due to the emotional and irrational concept of status, while the lower classes were unequipped for anything but emotional appeals, usually of a mystical nature. But the middle class developed as a result of its newly-emancipated right to the use of its reasoning power. It is no exaggeration to say that the major difference between a member of the middle class and a lower class peasant was the fact that the former had money and property, while the latter did not. A duke without money was an impoverished duke, but a merchant without money was a peasant. Thus, the merchant, lacking permanent status, relied upon his brain for survival, and supported endeavors which would increase his knowledge. The merchant class congregated near their markets in cities and here the philosophes found a ready audience. The Enlightenment appeal to reason was eagerly accepted by members of the rising middle class.

The men of the Enlightenment were a diverse group. All believed in progress and reason, but beyond that, there were as many differences as there were similarities. This was to be expected; after all, a key concept of the Enlightenment was individualism. Thus, more often than not, the appearance of any important work of the period would be applauded by some thinkers, and condemned by others. Voltaire and Rousseau were usually at odds with one another. Montesquieu called for a government based upon almost-mathematical laws, while Rousseau demanded rule by a mystical "general will" of the people. Almost, all Enlightenment figures criticized organized religion, but their alternatives varied. Voltaire was a Deist, believing in God but not in any organized church. Pierre Bayle, author of the *Critical and Historical Dictionary,* was a religious skeptic. Holbach became the father of modern atheism. On the other hand, Jansenism, an almost-Calvinist version of Catholicism, was most powerful during this period. The Quakers and Methodists can trace their origins to the Reformation, as can the mystical Swedenborgians. Pietism, a spiritual, other-worldly version of Christianity, swept the Germanys in this period. If one may use a Newtonian concept in the social sciences, it might be said that every Enlightenment idea had an equal and opposite reaction. One can almost discern an "anti-Enlightenment" movement flourishing side by side with the Enlightenment. Yet, can the critic really say that George Fox and John Wesley were leaders of this anti-movement? These founders of Quakerism and Methodism have left many writings, which mark them as true sons of the Enlightenment. And one can notice another quality which runs throughout all the religious developments of the period: a lessening of religious bigotry and superstition.

If there were apparent schisms in the area of religion, there were also important divisions in the study of economics. During the seventeenth century, the single most powerful group of economists were the mercantilists. These men held that a nation's wealth is measured in terms of gold, silver, and precious stones. A nation should export more than it imports in order to assure a "favorable balance of trade." Colonies were prized by mercantilists, both as sources of raw materials and markets for surpluses.

Eighteenth century economic theory represented a complete break from and rejection of mercantilism. Francois Quesnay saw in the circulation of the economy parallels to the circulation of blood in the human body; both were beneficial and should be encouraged. Quesnay was the leader of a group of economists known as the physiocrats. This group held that a nation's wealth is based on farming and mining, and that manufacturing and trading were not the creators of wealth, but the transformers and exchangers of it. Government restrictions, such as those of the mercantilists, hinder the free development of the economy, and should be held to an absolute minimum. Quesnay spoke of laissez-faire, or "let them do as they will," as the best policy toward the economy, one which would assure its growth and prosperity. Adam Smith was influenced by Quesnay and the physiocrats. *His Wealth of Nations*, published in 1776, was a persuasive argument in favor of the laissez-faire doctrines. Using reason, men such as these concluded that there were natural laws of economics; Smith was considered by many to be the Newton of economics. His ideas and those of the physiocrats were widespread among the philosophes. Jefferson in particular was influenced by them, as were other Americans of the Revolutionary generation.

Religion and economics were only two of the many areas influenced by the thinking of the philosophes. Indeed, there was scarcely an area of endeavor-from music to criminology to government-that was not influenced by their ideas.

Still, it is important to note that although the ideas of the philosophes were generally greeted by applause by the powers that be, few of them were actually put into practice. The philosophes argued that government should be rational. The enlightened despots listened politely, made token reforms, but retained the forms and policies of absolutism. Only Joseph of Austria attempted a full-scale program of reform, and his efforts ended with failure. The Church was attacked, but it remained strong. Despite the acceptance of the physiocrats' theories, mercantilism remained the dominant economic philosophy. Education scarcely changed; nor did the treatment of criminals. Thus, the men of the Enlightenment preached reason and progress, but saw irrationality still strangling Europe. Rousseau argued that only a violent revolution could change this situation. Montesquieu hoped that gradual changes would lead to a more enlightened government in France. Turgot was named Finance Minister to Louis XVI, but was dismissed when he tried to bring order out of the chaos of French fiscal policy.

The gap between theory and reality led to three reactions: Rousseau's revolutionism, Montesquieu's gradualism, and a third reaction, from those who denied the existence of a problem at all. The philosophical father of this last school of thought was Gottfried Wilhelm von Leibnitz (1646-1716). Leibnitz was a major philosopher and mathematician who, among his other accomplishments, is credited with the independent discovery of calculus. Although he died before the flowering of the Enlightenment, Leibnitz was an important influence on many of the later thinkers. Much of his philosophy stemmed from his attempts to prove the existence of God. Without going into details regarding his ideas, essentially Leibnitz, believed the universe was composed of "monads," each of which contained a spiritual as well as a physical aspect. From this Leibnitz attempted to prove the existence of God based on his conclusion that there is a pre-established harmony in the universe, which is God-made. Thus, he seems to have agreed with Newton: God is the great giver of mathematical laws, which operate throughout the universe for all time. Leibnitz and his followers were optimistic, as were most of the men of the Enlightenment. To them, this meant that all that happened was part of the world-plan of a mechanistic God. Leibnitz did not say so, but some of his followers concluded that as a result, this is the best of all possible worlds. Progress is assured; all that happens is for the good; perfection is within the grasp of those who harmonize their actions with the laws of God.

One of those who came to this conclusion was the third Earl of Shaftesbury. "Oh glorious nature, supremely fair and sovereignly good," he wrote. Nature is always good; if it appears evil, the fault lies within us for being unable to see the grand design. To Shaftesbury, all nature conspired for the general good.

This view was seconded by Alexander Pope, one of the most important poets of the Enlightenment. In his influential *Essay on Man*, Pope wrote:

All Nature is but Art, unknown to thee; All Chance, Direction, which thou canst not see; All Discord, Harmony not understood; All partial evil, universal Good; And, spite of Pride, in erring Reason's spite One truth is clear, Whatever is, is right.

Needless to say, individuals such as these, content to see nothing but good around them, were hardly apt to become reformers. Is it any wonder, then, that they were viewed with contempt by those philosophes engaged in reform activities? These extreme optimists were the targets of many attacks from those who saw a disparity between man's knowledge and his accomplishments. The most savage and biting of these came from Francois-Marie Arouet, who wrote under the name of Voltaire.

VOLTAIRE

Francois-Marie Arouet (he took the pen name de Voltaire at the age of twenty-three) was born into a middle class French family on November 21, 1694. Voltaire's father was a lawyer, whose clients included such famous families as that of the Duke of Sully and Cardinal Richelieu. The father was also a Jansenist, professing a variety of Catholicism based on the teachings of St. Augustine, which stressed "grace" rather than "works." The Jansenist moral code was as strict as that of the Calvinists, and so we may assume that Voltaire's early years were spent in an authoritarian environment. Voltaire's mother died when he was seven years old, and at this point the harsh code of his father became oppressive.

At the age of ten, Voltaire was sent away to a Jesuit school. It is difficult to understand why the father sent him to a school run by the theological enemies of the Jansenists; perhaps it was because the Jesuits were considered the best teachers of the time. In any case, the school was even more authoritarian than his home. Voltaire later wrote that he was grateful for the education and work habits the Order instilled in him, but he revolted against the harsh discipline at the time. He left school at the age of sixteen, intent on spending his life writing. His father considered such pursuits useless, and tried to interest his son-in-law. When Voltaire refused to enter law school, he was sent to Paris. Then, in 1713, he was named to a junior diplomatic post at The Hague. Voltaire entered the gay life of the sophisticated city; when his father learned of this, he warned his son to repent or be sent to the wilds of America. Still, Voltaire continued to frequent the salons, and began to write poetry. He eventually returned to Paris, and became a minor luminary during the wild, hedonistic days of the Regency (the period after the death of Louis XIV and before the coming of age of Louis XV). He was banished from Paris and for a while imprisoned for having written some barbed **satires** directed at the Regent.

In 1718, the twenty-four year old Voltaire wrote *Oedipe,* a tragedy, which was his first successful work. Others followed, and Voltaire was soon considered an important French playwright. In 1723 he wrote a play whose hero was Henry IV, who brought unity and religious peace to France. Soon after his career took a turn for the worse. Voltaire argued with the Chevalier de Rohan, was badly beaten by Rohan's men, and hospitalized. He challenged Rohan to a duel, but was arrested and placed in the Bastille before the two men could meet on the field of honor. He was allowed to leave on condition that he go to England. Thus, in 1726, Voltaire crossed the Channel, and stayed in England until 1729.

Voltaire later wrote that his stay in England was one of the most important periods of his life. London seemed free after the harsh days in Paris; the Englishman of the eighteenth century appeared to have many more freedoms than his French counterpart. While in England he wrote his *Philosophical Letters*, which praised England and criticized France. The book was published in 1734, after Voltaire had returned to Paris. It was burned, and a warrant was issued for the author's arrest. This time Voltaire was prepared for the attack. Wealthy as a result of several successful books, he fled France and went to the independent Duchy of Lorraine where he lived at a chateau with his mistress, Emilie, the Marquise du Chatelet, and her most accommodating husband.

Voltaire was able to return to France in 1744, and became a member of the Royal Court. But he was unhappy in France, and in 1750 finally accepted an appointment to the court of Frederick the Great which had been offered to him on several occasions in the past. But the two men were both individualists, and in short order they quarreled and were no longer on speaking terms. Accordingly, Voltaire left Frederick's employ and, in 1753, returned to France.

The stay in France was to be short; Voltaire's enemies were still in power, and he was forced to leave again. The author's next home was Geneva, which he liked insofar as climate was concerned, but disliked because of its authoritarian Calvinistic atmosphere. In 1758 he purchased a large estate near Ferny, on French soil but within a few miles of Geneva. At the time he was sixty-four years old. Voltaire, "the Patriarch of Ferny," was also known as "the hotel keeper of Europe," as the great thinkers of the time made pilgrimages to his home and often stayed for long visits. From time to time Voltaire would venture from his home, but never for long. In 1778, at the age of eighty-four, he died in Paris.

VOLTAIRE'S PHILOSOPHY AND CANDIDE

It is difficult to generalize about a man whose writings cover more than sixty years of time and fill over seventy large volumes. Still, there are some basic ideas to be found in all of his works.

Voltaire was a passionate defender of freedom. His most famous quote is: "I do not agree with a word that you say, but I will defend to the death your right to say it." Throughout his life, he defended the rights of men to write and say what they wished. On the other hand, he sometimes was intolerant in his criticisms of his enemies.

Voltaire was a believer in and practitioner of the historical method. This can best be seen in one of his major works, The

Age of Louis XIV (1756). In it, Voltaire is not only interested in the parade of leading figures, as many of his predecessors had been, but in the lives of the people, the "temper of the times," and in casual relationships. Some modern historians credit Voltaire with having been the first to use the term "philosophy of history." In his works, we find none of the supernatural events which mark previous histories. Voltaire once wrote that it is impossible to verify events before the fifteenth century, which indicates his interest in sources and the use of historical criticism. On the other hand, some of the material found in his works cannot be verified independently.

Voltaire was anti-clerical as a natural outgrowth of his belief in freedom and the historical method. He saw no basis in fact for the claims of the various churches and charged religious leaders with suppressing free thought and criticism. Referring to the clergy, he wrote, "Crush the infamous thing!" As for himself, Voltaire was a Deist, and is often considered the father of the movement.

Voltaire believed in rule by reason. He was no democrat, having little trust in the common man. Voltaire called for rule by an enlightened despot, who would allow freedom of speech and other basic freedoms, and do what had to be done, not that which was popular with the masses. It was for this reason, among others, that Frederick the Great admired Voltaire. It may be said that Voltaire desired freedom for the enlightened, and cared little for the rest of humanity.

As important as these contributions were, Voltaire's major impact was due to other factors, namely his catalytic qualities and his skepticism.

Voltaire was the major intellectual influence during much of the French Enlightenment. This influence came not only from his own writings, but also through his work with others. The Encyclopedists considered him their leader; the physiocrats thought of Voltaire as their guide. Turgot turned to Voltaire, then an old man, when he gained power in French politics. His writing influenced an entire generation of French Revolutionaries. During his later life, Voltaire had a long correspondence with Rousseau. Although the two men differed on many points, the impact of Voltaire on Rousseau is evident from reading the letters.

The fact that Voltaire always considered himself more a critic than anything else is probably why many have said that he was more destructive than constructive. Such criticisms of Voltaire ignore his writings which praise the English constitution, his defense of religious freedom in France and elsewhere, and his programs for reform. True, these make up only a small fraction of the man's total output, but they are there nonetheless.

Voltaire looked around him and saw rampant irrationality. The thinkers of the Enlightenment put forth their programs, but they had little effect during the reigns of Louis XV and Louis XVI. Voltaire considered it to be his function to observe the stupidities of society, and to point out necessary changes. Where other major Enlightenment figures, such as Montesquieu and Rousseau, wrote of grandiose schemes for a universal amelioration of the human condition-and did little concrete about it-Voltaire called for specific reforms. If his approach was piecemeal, it had the virtue of being more realistic. Rousseau called for freedom of religion; Voltaire risked his very life in defending a Protestant, Jean Calas, who was convicted of a crime more for his religion than for his actual guilt. Rousseau called for a sweeping away of all religions; Voltaire was more circumspect. In writing to Frederick the Great, he said:

As long as there are fools and knaves there will be religion. Ours is the most ridiculous, the most absurd, and the most bloody that has ever infected the world. Your Majesty will do the human race an eternal service in extirpating this infamous superstition. I do not say among the rabble, who are not worthy of being enlightened and who are apt for every yoke; I say among the well bred, among those who think, among those who wish to think. Their number is not very great.

If we read between the biting lines, we can see a sharp insight into the problems of the times. Some philosophes believed that once the individual realized that his life was irrational, he would give up his old ways completely to accept the new, rational way of life. Voltaire realized that the "average man" was not prepared for such a change, even if it were possible. Therefore, he called for freedom-but only for those who knew how to handle it.

To this end, Voltaire believed in education; he agreed with Locke's idea of a tabula rasa. Faulty education was a major problem; better education would solve many of the difficulties facing mankind. Why do we call ourselves Christians? Because we were educated to think of ourselves as such. In Zaire, Voltaire has a Moslem girl proclaim:

Custom and law alone, applied in early youth, Have caused me to believe that Islam is the truth. I see it all, the bent of children's education, Makes their belief and thoughts cherished by the nation. Were I an Indian, a false God I should fear, A Christian girl in France, a faithful Moslem here.

Voltaire saved the sharpest arrows in his quiver for those who refused to see the problems and injustices of the modern world. Among these were those philosophes who proclaimed the optimism of Leibnitz, but actually had perverted his philosophy.

His mistress, Emilie, was one of these; she saw God's purpose in all things, including the many evils which surrounded her beautiful chateau. Voltaire was gentle with her, and did not poke fun at Emilie's beliefs. But ten years after her death, in 1758, he wrote *Candide,* a biting **satire** about these optimists, and what many consider to be his greatest work.

Candide is a work of the eighteenth century in many respects. In the first place, its philosophy is that of the Enlightenment; it is a work by a man of reason. Secondly, it is historical in tone; most of the material presented in the **satire** is based on actual occurrences. Finally, it is pure Voltaire: biting, insinuating, subtle (though at times direct), and sharp. Voltaire criticizes the Europe of his time in many of the chapters, but his greatest scorn is reserved for those who, having the intelligence, refuse to see what to him is obvious. For example, one of the great disasters of the century was the Lisbon earthquake, in which thousands perished. Yet, some philosophes saw God's plan even in this tragedy. The earthquake is discussed in *Candide,* but in his Poem on the *Disaster of Lisbon,* written two years earlier, Voltaire was even more biting:

The heirs of the dead would now come into their fortunes, masons would grow rich in rebuilding the city, beasts would grow fat on corpses buried in the ruins; such is the natural effect of natural causes. So don't worry about your own particular evil; you are contributing to the general good.

The poem was the chief item of conversation in the salons that season. The city fathers of Geneva, shocked at its implications, wrote to Rousseau, asking him to reply to and refute Voltaire. Rousseau agreed, and published an article in which he said that the disaster was man's fault, and not God's. Had men not been living in cities, which were unnatural, they would have been spared the horrors of Lisbon. Then Rousseau turned his pen to his old friend, Voltaire, and wrote: "May heaven keep me from offending the one of my contemporaries whose talents I esteem most deeply; but here it is destiny that is in question, destiny on which I stake everything."

Voltaire did not answer this letter; he knew full well that his opponents and those of Rousseau would like nothing better than to see the two fighting. But his reply did come, taking another form: two years later he wrote *Candide*.

In 1758 Voltaire journeyed to visit the Elector of the Palatinate, who had promised him an annuity for the rest of his life. While traveling, he was given hospitality by several princes who lived along the way. Voltaire rested for a while at a castle belonging to the Margrave of Baden-Durlach, in Karlsruhe. It was there that he began to plan *Candide*.

Tradition has it that Voltaire wrote *Candide* in four days, during which time he was locked in his room, the door closed except to receive food and coffee. On the fourth day he emerged, gave the manuscript to his niece, and said: "Here, curious Madame, is something you may read."

For some time Voltaire, who had become quite wealthy, had published some of his works anonymously, or under pseudonyms. This was to be the case with *Candide*, on whose title page was inscribed: "Translated from the German by Dr. Ralph." He wrote to his friends, denying the authorship of the work. "What sort of work is this *Candide*, of which it is said that it is scandal to sell it, and which is supposed to have originated in Lyons? I might like to have it. Couldn't you, gentlemen, get me a bound copy? It is said that some people are brazen enough to claim that I am the author of this work, which I have never laid eyes on."

Voltaire gave himself away, forever, when the Calvinist leaders of Geneva banned the book, and had it publicly burned. He wrote several scathing anti-religious tracts, and had them distributed in the city. After that, he didn't deny authorship of *Candide*.

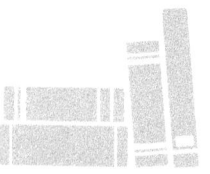

CANDIDE

TEXTUAL ANALYSIS

CHAPTERS 1 - 7

....

CHAPTER ONE: HOW CANDIDE WAS BROUGHT UP IN A BEAUTIFUL COUNTRY HOUSE, AND HOW HE WAS DRIVEN AWAY

Candide, a fine young man, lived in Westphalia, at the country seat of Baron Thunder-ten-tronckh. He was called Candide (candid) because of his "unaffected simplicity." The Baron was probably the boy's uncle. Candide was not recognized as his nephew, however, perhaps because his suspected father could only list seventy-one ancestors.

The Baron was the most important man in the state; "they all called him Your Lordship, and laughed at his jokes." The Baroness was very fat, and so was considered very important. Her daughter, Cunegonde, was quite beautiful. The family's tutor, Dr. Pangloss, was an authority on all matters, and was admired by Candide. Pangloss taught "metaphysico-theologo-cosmolo-nigology." "He proved incontestably that there is no effect without a cause, and that in this best of all possible worlds, his lordship's country seat was the most beautiful of mansions and her ladyship was the best of all possible ladyships. All things were made for a purpose. Noses were made to carry glasses, and so we have glasses. Legs were intended for pants, and so we wear pants."

Candide believed Pangloss and loved Cunegonde. One day Cunegonde saw Pangloss flirting with a waiting-woman. His "teachings" led her to desire Candide. Then the two kissed. The Baron witnessed this, drove Candide from the house, and boxed Cunegonde's ears.

Comment

Voltaire wrote in spare prose, but each sentence sparkles with wit. In this introductory chapter we meet Candide, and are immediately told that he **represents simplicity**. He is the type of hero "to whom things happen." In other words, **Voltaire will develop his ideas by presenting the world through Candide's eyes**. Candide is the perennial boy who says the Emperor is wearing no clothes; he is innocence incarnate. To a lesser extent, so is Cunegonde. Voltaire pokes fun at the nobility in his descriptions of the Baron and Baroness. But his **satire** is directed primarily at Pangloss. Here is the pretentious philosophe, who claims to encompass all knowledge in his teachings; the pseudo-scientist who is not above making a pass at a servant-girl. **Pangloss' philosophy is a perversion of Leibnitz' teachings, and resembles those of Pope and Shaftesbury**. He claims this is the best of all possible worlds, and perceives a good purpose in all that occurs. We will see his reasoning develop as the book progresses. Voltaire tells us that Pangloss is Candide's teacher. Thus, innocence will be shown that the brutality of the world is really good in disguise.

CHAPTER TWO: WHAT HAPPENED TO CANDIDE AMONGST THE BULGARS

Candide was dejected as he wandered away from the Baron's castle. The next day, cold and hungry, he stopped at an inn in the nearby town of Waldberghoff-trarbk-dikdorff. There he met two men dressed in blue uniforms who were recruiting officers, and saw in Candide a potential soldier. They invited him to dine, and asked Candide if he admired the Bulgar King. Candide said he didn't know the King. The soldiers asked Candide to drink to the King's health anyway, which he did. The soldiers considered this to be an avowal of support and an enlistment in the Bulgar Army. "You are now his support and defender," they said, "and a Bulgar hero in the bargain. Your fortune is made. Go where glory waits you." With this, Candide was clapped into irons and taken to the barracks. He was taught the manual of arms and given thirty lashes. The training continued the next day, at which time Candide was given twenty lashes. The third day he received only ten. Candide thus showed remarkable progress, and was considered a fine soldier.

Candide did not like the military life, and tried to desert. He was captured, and after a court martial was given the choice of being shot twelve times in the brain or being flogged thirty-six times by the entire regiment. Candide believed in free will, and wanted to say that he chose neither, but he had to pick one of the alternatives. Exercising his liberty, he chose the floggings. After running the regiment twice, and having received 4,000 blows, he was near death. Candide begged to be beheaded and the soldiers decided to grant him that favor.

Just as he was about to be killed, the Bulgar King passed by, and asked about Candide's crime. Recognizing that Candide was a philosopher, and ignorant of the ways of the world, he decided to grant him a pardon, "an act of mercy which will be praised in every newspaper and in every age." Candide was just about healed of his wounds when a war broke out between the Bulgars and the Abars.

Comment

Candide's encounter at the inn is the first time our hero-a believer in logic and reason-comes face to face with the real world. He is "bilked" by the recruiting officers: praised for his patriotism, told he is a hero, and then taken to camp in chains. So much for the glory of military life! In camp, progress is measured by the fact that Candide receives less punishment each day of training. In this section, Voltaire views the world through the eyes of Pangloss. He implies that Candide should be proud and happy to have progressed to the point where he is receiving only ten lashes! But Candide, being innocent, does not realize this, and attempts to flee. He is captured, put on trial, and then given his choice of two methods of death. So much for the doctrine of free will as expounded by the optimists of the Enlightenment. Can such a choice ever be free? Candide elects to be flogged, and after two runs through the regiment, pleads for the mercy of death. Voltaire says that the soldiers decide to grant this request, and so shows the hypocrisy of the modern world. It is an act of mercy to behead a man! In addition, Voltaire shows the nature of bureaucratic thinking; it never occurs to anyone that Candide may not have to be killed at all. Our hero is finally saved by the King of the Bulgars, who most students of the book recognize as Frederick the Great. Candide is pardoned, for as a philosopher, he cannot be expected to know anything. Thus, Voltaire dismisses those philosophes who spend their time thinking, but have never bothered to observe the world around them.

CHAPTER THREE: HOW CANDIDE ESCAPED FROM THE BULGARS, AND WHAT HAPPENED TO HIM AFTERWARDS

The author opens by describing the grandeurs of two armies preparing for combat. Quite casually, he mentions that the opening salvo from the artillery killed about twelve thousand men. Then nine or ten thousand are killed by rifle fire. Bayonet attacks account for several thousand more. The total deaths were about thirty thousand. Candide was no hero-and as Voltaire implies, no fool-he "trembled like a philosopher, and hid himself as best he could during this heroic butchery."

The rival kings celebrate their victories (Voltaire reveals that each considered the carnage to be a victory for his own side) with Te Deums. Candide decides to investigate the results of the battle, and goes into the battlefield, reaching a village on the Abar side of the border. The village was ruined, "for the Bulgars had burned it to the ground in accordance with the terms of international law." The dead and wounded were everywhere.

Then Candide goes to a Bulgar village, and sees the same misery and destruction there. He continues to walk, and is soon away from the war zone. He enters Holland, hungry and thinking of Cunegonde. Candide has heard that the Dutch are rich and Christian; he feels he will be treated well in Holland. Yet, when he asks some passers-by for bread, they tell him that he will be sent to a reformatory if he continues to beg.

Candide then approaches a group which is being addressed by an orator on the subject of charity. The orator asks if Candide supports "the Good Old Cause." Like a philosopher, Candide replies that there is no effect without a cause and that all is arranged for the best, feeling he was destined to be driven from Cunegonde and undergo the torments of the past few days. The orator does not understand this, and asks Candide if he thinks the Pope is an Antichrist. Our hero replies that he has never heard anyone say so, and in any case, he wants some food. The orator-a minister-says that Candide does not deserve to eat, and threatens him with harm unless he leaves. The minister's wife is not so charitable; on hearing that Candide is not sure the Pope is an Antichrist, she empties a pot filled with an undescribed substance on his head, "which shows to what lengths ladies are driven by religious zeal." James, an Anabaptist who had never been christened, takes pity on Candide, takes him home, washes and feeds him, and then offers him a job manufacturing "those Persian silks that are made in Holland." Candide is grateful; Pangloss was right, and all is for the best in the world.

Candide meets a beggar covered with sores the next day. The beggar is in poor condition and coughs violently.

Comment

Voltaire opens by describing the beauties of armies and the horrors of war. This kind of juxtaposition was one of Voltaire's favorite devices; he uses it throughout Candide and it can be found in his other works of **satire**. He then tells of the casualties of battle, and notes that Candide hid throughout the conflict. Voltaire considers this to be the only course of action open to a wise man in time of war. If war is stupid-and Voltaire believes it is-then why fight? (It is interesting to note that Bertrand Russell has given the same advice to the young men of today. If and when a new war comes, Russell counseled, hide and save yourselves, for you will be needed to reconstruct the world after the barbarians kill themselves.) Voltaire continues, taking Candide on a tour of the battlefields after the fighting ends. He describes scenes of horror in towns burned under the strict regulations adhering to international law, again indicating his contempt of the bureaucratic mind. Then Candide goes to Holland, expecting to find the people there Christian in temper. He is told to stop begging and go about his business. Christ called for love and charity, by the eighteenth century Christian apparently has little of either to dispense. This **allusion** is fortified by the **episode** of the preacher and his wife. These dedicated people of the cloth treat Candide most shabbily. Voltaire is especially scornful of the wife. Her crime is that of fanaticism. A fanatic for Christ can be the most bigoted and un-Christian of people. Candide is finally saved by a man who was not baptized, but is the first person of decent inclinations we meet in the book. He is apparently a merchant, and even here Voltaire cannot suppress a dig. His business is producing Persian silks-in Holland! Yet, through this all, Candide remains the optimist.

CHAPTER FOUR: HOW CANDIDE MET HIS OLD TUTOR, DR. PANGLOSS AND WHAT CAME OF IT

Candide feels sorry for the old beggar, and he gives him some coins that James had given him. Then, the beggar begins to hug Candide, who shrinks in horror and then surprise. It appears that the old beggar is none other than Dr. Pangloss! Candide leads his old teacher to the Anabaptist's stable, gives him some food, and asks about Cunegonde. He is told that Cunegonde is dead, disemboweled by Bulgar soldiers who first raped her repeatedly. The Baron and Baroness were killed when they tried to defend her; the Baron had his head broken while the Baroness was cut into small pieces. The Bulgars also destroyed the castle, in revenge for an Abar destruction of a Bulgar castle. With this, Candide faints.

When Candide recovers, he asks how it is that Pangloss has been reduced to such a pitiful state in this best of all possible worlds. Pangloss replies it is because of love. He had enjoyed Paquette, the serving-girl at the palace. Alas, she had venereal disease! Pangloss is infected with it. It seems that Paquette got it from a learned Franciscan, who showed his learning by tracing it back to its source, one of the companions of Christopher Columbus. The line will end with Pangloss, who fears he is dying.

Candide asks if the devil is behind all this. Pangloss replies that this is not the case. If Columbus had not visited the West Indies, where the disease was contracted, we would not have chocolate or cochineal. The disease, like religious wars, is a European malady; it has not infected other people.

Candide says that a cure must be found; Pangloss replies he has no money for doctors, and none will cure him without a fee. Candide tells James about Pangloss, and the good Anabaptist agrees to pay for the cure: Pangloss is saved, and loses only an eye and an ear. He then takes employment as accountant for the Anabaptist.

Two months later the three men take a business trip to Lisbon. While on board the ship, Pangloss and James discuss Pangloss' belief that all is for the best. James disagrees with this and argues that God may have meant this to be the case, but man has changed it. Man was not intended to be a wolf, yet he acts like one. God did not give men guns, yet man made them and has destroyed, killed, and maimed his fellow-creatures. Pangloss has a ready answer. These are more examples of his belief in progress. These misfortunes contribute to the general good, and so the more misfortunes there are, the better things will be! While the two men discuss the question, the ship is caught in a terrible storm, just in sight of Lisbon.

Comment

On meeting Candide, Pangloss tells him of the death of Cunegonde and her parents. They have been killed in the Bulgar-Abar Wa- which appears to be the Seven Years' War. Candide cannot understand how Pangloss can remain optimistic, considering his present state of disease and starvation. Pangloss replies that Candide cannot see the whole picture. With the use of Liebniz' philosophy, he argues that while it is true that there are apparent wrongs in the world, when placed in the total context, they will be seen as the good. It seems true that Pangloss would not have venereal disease if Columbus had not gone to the West Indies. But if he had not gone there, then Europe would not have chocolate. Pangloss then makes an invidious comparison between venereal disease and religious wars: both are European maladies. Thus, Voltaire indicates his contempt of organized religion. While on the ship to Lisbon, James and Pangloss argue the question of apparent evil in a world that is supposedly good. In this discussion, Pangloss refuses to allow himself to be dissuaded by James' request to look at the world. He says, in effect, "Don't bother me with facts; I've made up my mind."

CHAPTER FIVE: DESCRIBING TEMPEST, SHIPWRECK, AND EARTHQUAKE, AND WHAT HAPPENED TO DR. PANGLOSS, CANDIDE, AND JAMES, THE ANABAPTIST

Half the passengers on the ship became sick during the storm, while the other half cried and said their prayers. The ship seemed on the verge of sinking. James tried to help direct the ship, and was struck down by an excited sailor, who fell into the sea as a result of his fear. James assisted the sailor when he climbed back aboard the ship, but he himself was pitched into the sea as a result of his efforts. The sailor, now safe, did nothing to help him. Candide saw James go down, and wanted to jump into the sea to save him. He was stopped by Pangloss, who tried to prove that Lisbon harbor was built in order for James to drown there. While Pangloss weaved his philosophical discourse, the ship split in two. All were lost, except Candide, Pangloss, and the sailor whom James had saved. The three men were washed ashore. When they had recovered sufficiently, they started toward town.

As they reached Lisbon, the earth began to tremble, and the sea in the harbor began to boil, destroying many ships. The entire city was leveled by the earthquake, and thirty thousand people died in the ruins.

The sailor chuckled, and remarked that Lisbon was ripe for looting. Pangloss asked what the reason for the phenomenon might be. Candide thought the Day of Judgement had come.

The sailor rushed into the city and began looting. He then got drunk, found a prostitute whom he paid with some of the stolen money, and slept with her among the ruins. Pangloss tried to stop him, saying that the sailor was not obeying the rule of reason. The sailor was contemptuous of this advice and stated he was born in Batavia, in the East Indies, and had trampled on the crucifix four times on his trips to Japan. "I'm not the man for your Universal Reason."

Meanwhile, Candide had fallen in the rubble, wounded by masonry splinters. He called to Pangloss, asking for wine and oil for his last rites. But Pangloss ignored the plea, and spoke of the earthquake instead. It was not a new earthquake, he said; Lima, Peru, had a similar disaster, and Pangloss believed there was a vein of sulphur running between that city and Lisbon. Candide didn't agree, and renewed his cry for wine and oil. Pangloss ignored the request, and restated his belief that the two earthquakes were interconnected. Candide lost consciousness, and Pangloss revived him with water from a nearby fountain.

The next day, Pangloss and Candide found some food among the ruins and satisfied their hunger. Some of those they had helped gave them a meal, and all cried while they ate. Pangloss tried to cheer them up; things could not be otherwise, he said. The earthquake was a manifestation of the correctness of things, he maintained. If there was a volcano at Lisbon, it could be nowhere else. Things cannot be anywhere except where they are, for everything is for the best.

A member of the Inquisition heard this, and approached Pangloss. He said that it appeared as though Pangloss did not believe in original sin; "for if all is for the best, there can be no such thing as the fall of Man and eternal punishment." Pangloss disagreed; while it was certainly true that Man had fallen from grace, the fall itself was for the best, being part of the divine scheme of the universe. The member of the Inquisition then asked Pangloss whether he believed in Free Will. Pangloss answered that Free Will was consistent with all he had said. It was ordained that we should be free. As he spoke, the officer turned to a henchman, who was then occupied with pouring him a glass of port wine.

Comment

There are two parts to this chapter, and two messages. The first is concerned with James and the sailor; the second with the earthquake and its results. Note that James, who was not baptized, saves his fellow man. The sailor, presumably a Christian, is ungrateful and acts in a disgraceful manner. When

Pangloss tries to reason with the sailor, he is rebuffed; the sailor will have nothing to do with Universal Reason. So much for the nature of the "common man." To Voltaire, he is an ungrateful animal, who is incapable of good, and acts by his emotions, and not his brain. He says he does not desire Reason, and Voltaire seems to agree. The author, unlike many of the philosophes (especially Rousseau) does not glorify the common man. To Rousseau, the noble savage was the best hope of the world; to Voltaire, he was for more savage than noble. The importance of the Lisbon Earthquake to Voltaire and other philosophes has already been discussed. It dealt a shattering blow to the optimism of the mid-eighteenth century. Pangloss voices a rather weak defense of God's will in the midst of this disaster - a caricature of the Leibnitz position on such matters. The **satire** of this chapter and the others dealing with the Lisbon Earthquake was directed more at Rousseau than anyone else. Rousseau said that man must learn to be patient and endure the unendurable. Evil is the result of his own nature and the nature of the universe. He intimates that God has done the best he can by man, and man must learn to live with what he has. Voltaire responds in Candide by asking why an omnipotent, benevolent God would let such things as the Lisbon Earthquake occur. He would agree with Rousseau's view as to the depravity of man, but could not accept the younger man's views on the nature of God.

CHAPTER SIX: HOW A MAGNIFICENT AUTO-DA-FE WAS STAGED TO PREVENT FURTHER EARTHQUAKES, AND HOW CANDIDE WAS FLOGGED

The authorities at the University of Coimbra decided that the burning of a few people would prevent future earthquakes. Thus, an auto-da-fe was planned. (An auto-da-fe is an "act of faith." In the Middle Ages they usually took the form of burning heretics at the stake and other killings and tortures. In some ways, they resembled the sacrifices ancient people made to their deities. In others, they were a manifestation of the scape goat theory, in which the person to be sacrificed took upon himself the sins of the community, and his death absolved the community of its collective guilt.)

The authorities searched for suitable candidates for the sacrifice. They found a Basque who was convicted of marrying his godmother, and two Portuguese Jews who refused to eat bacon. Pangloss and Candide were also taken; Pangloss had said that the earthquake was all for the best, and Candide had listened to him. They were taken to a jail "where they suffered no inconvenience from the sun." Thus, they languished in a dark dungeon until they were dressed in ceremonial garb and taken to be executed. They heard a moving sermon and beautiful music; Candide was flogged in time to the anthems. Their companions were burned and Pangloss was hung. But on the same day, apparently after the sacrifices, another earthquake occurred. Candide could not understand this. If this is the best of all worlds, what are the others like? Were all the horrible things that had happened to him really necessary? An old woman then stopped him and asked Candide to follow her.

Comment

In this short chapter, Voltaire shows the monstrousness of some religious activities. Christians burn their fellow men at the stake, and Candide is flogged in time to a hymn of praise to God. Candide cannot understand this, and questions his beliefs.

CHAPTER SEVEN: HOW AN OLD WOMAN TOOK CARE OF CANDIDE, AND HOW HE FOUND THE LADY HE LOVED

It was difficult for Candide to compose himself, but he followed the old woman, who took him to her home and fed him. He tried to thank her, but she went away without saying more, only bidding him to eat, rest, and rub himself with ointment. Candide did all of these things.

When the old woman returned the next day, Candide asked why she was so kind. She did not reply, and again left. In the evening she returned, and told Candide to follow her. He was taken to a house on the outskirts of town, and shown into a richly decorated bedroom. Then she left him alone. Shortly she returned, and with her was a veiled Cunegonde. The young people were overcome with joy. After a while, Candide questioned her. He had been told by Pangloss that she had been ravished and disemboweled. Was this not true? Cunegonde said it was so, but people don't always die of such things. Her parents and brother had been killed, however. Then Candide asked what she was doing in Portugal, and in this house. Why did she have him brought here? Cunegonde promises to answer all of his questions, but first wanted to know what had happened to him. Candide then related his sad story. When he had finished, she began her tale.

Comment

This chapter serves as an introduction to the story of Cunegonde's adventures, which in some ways resemble those of *Candide*. The reader should note that Cunegonde, who was described as dead in a previous chapter, reappears suddenly and dramatically. Voltaire uses this device on several occasions in the book. This was an artistic device used by other writers of the time; Voltaire carries it to an extreme, thus satirizing some of his contemporaries. In general, the intent of *Candide* is not to tell a story, but to present a dramatized attack on a philosophical school. Voltaire feels free to take such liberties with his story, if they serve this purpose.

CANDIDE

TEXTUAL ANALYSIS

CHAPTERS 8 - 14

CHAPTER EIGHT: CUNEGONDE'S STORY

In this chapter, Cunegonde describes her adventures since she has last seen Candide. Like him, she is an optimist. While Candide arrived at his optimism through Pangloss' philosophy, Cunegonde is more of a believer in the old Christian dogma that God is all-good and all-powerful, and therefore evil cannot exist.

One night, while she slept, the Bulgars (by the grace of God) arrived at Thunder-ten-tronckh. They murdered her family. One tall Bulgar, seeing her faint, began to rape her. Cunegonde recovered at this, and began to fight her attacker. Such goings on were by no means usual at Thunder-ten-tronckh. She was wounded on the left thigh, and still has a scar. (Candide sympathizes, and asks to see the scar. Cunegonde promises that he shall.)

A Bulgar captain came upon the struggling pair, and killed the soldier. He then had Cunegonde washed and taken to his quarters as a prisoner-of-war. She took care of his washing and such. The captain was handsome but was no philosopher; he had not been brought up by Pangloss.

After a while the captain ran out of funds and grew tired of Cunegonde, whom he sold to Don Issacher, a Jew who had a weakness for women. The Jew tried to ravish Cunegonde, but she defended her honor. "A woman of honor can be ravished once, but the experience is a tonic to her virtue." To make Cunegonde more cooperative, Don Issacher took her to his country home, where they settled down. (Cunegonde notes that this is where they are now. The country home, she thinks, is every bit as nice as Thunder-ten-tronckh.)

One day the Grand Inquisitor saw Cunegonde at mass, and asked to meet her. Cunegonde was then taken to his palace, where she told the Grand Inquisitor of her situation. She was shown that it is degrading to belong to a Jew. The Grand Inquisitor asked Don Issacher to give Cunegonde to him; the Jew, who was a court banker, refused. Then Don Issacher was threatened with an auto-da-fe. The Jew relented, and entered into an agreement with the Grand Inquisitor whereby the two men would share Cunegonde and the house between them. Don Issacher was to get both on Mondays, Wednesdays, and Saturdays (the Jewish sabbath). The agreement lasted for six months, but then the two men quarreled over whether Saturday was the Jew's because of the Old Testament or the Inquisitor's because of the New Testament. Cunegonde resisted both men, and so they both desired her.

After a while, the Grand Inquisitor invited Cunegonde to an auto-da-fe. This was the same ceremony in which Candide was to have been killed. She was shocked to see Pangloss there, and when he was hanged, she fainted. On recovering, she saw Candide, standing stark naked. She was distressed (Candide was handsomer that the Bulgar captain). Before she could speak, Candide was flogged. Cunegonde asked herself what could have brought Candide to Lisbon, to be hanged at the orders of the Grand Inquisitor. She doubted Pangloss; is this really the best of all worlds?

Cunegonde was frantic at the thought of Candide's being executed. She thought of many things, but mostly of the kiss Candide had given her at Thunder-ten-tronckh. That is why she ordered her old servant to bring Candide to her home.

The two lovers were hungry, and so ate their meal on the lovely couch on which they sat. They were enjoying each other when Don Issacher arrived on the scene.

Comment

Cunegonde's story is straight-forward, whereas Candide's contains many reflections. This is Voltaire's way of saying that women are much more realistic than men. Note that she says that the Grand Inquisitor and Don Issacher both want her, and this was so because she has withheld her favors from both men. This line is thrown out without elaboration; Cunegonde assumes that all will realize that this is part of the native wisdom of women. Cunegonde seems simple and unaffected, but underneath all of this is a wily female. Her problems have been as great as those of Candide, but her life has been easy, while he has suffered many injuries. When they meet, she is an honored guest at the auto-da-fe; Candide is the victim. Voltaire seems to be saying that it is wiser to be less of a philosopher and more of an opportunist for the sake of survival.

CHAPTER NINE: RELATING FURTHER ADVENTURES OF CUNEGONDE, CANDIDE, THE GRAND INQUISITOR, AND THE JEW

Issacher was distressed at seeing the two lovers together. He asked whether Cunegonde felt obliged to share her favors with one and all, drew out a dagger and attacked Candide. Our hero had been given a sword by the old woman, however, and he unsheathed it and killed the Jew. "Holy Virgin," Cunegonde exclaimed (in a most modern tone). "What will happen to us now? A man killed in my house! If the police come, we are done for."

Candide regrets the death of Pangloss; the philosopher would have given them good advice if he were alive. In his absence, they decide to consult the old woman. She was about to speak when the door opened, and in walked the Grand Inquisitor. Candide's mind worked quickly. If the Inquisitor called for help, both he and Cunegonde would be burnt at the stake. The Inquisitor had had Candide whipped, and besides, he was a rival and must be eliminated. Without giving the matter more thought, Candide killed the Grand Inquisitor.

Cunegonde bewails their fate; they will now surely be excommunicated. Candide has killed a Jew and a priest in less than two minutes. Our hero replies that a man in love doesn't know what he is doing, especially if he has been whipped by the Inquisition.

The old woman then gives her advice. They must take the horses in the stable and flee., Cunegonde must be sure to take her jewels with her. The three mount the horses and make off for Cadiz.

Shortly after they left the house, the police arrived. The Inquisitor was buried in a beautiful church, while the Jew was thrown on a dunghill. Meanwhile Candide, Cunegonde, and the old woman reached the small town of Avacena, and went to an inn there.

Comment

Having finished with the **episode** in Lisbon, Voltaire must find a way to remove his hero to another location, and another moral and story. Thus, he has him kill Cunegonde's two patrons and flee to Cadiz, an important port of embarkation for the New World. Note the differing reactions of *Candide* and Cunegonde to the murders (or killings). The woman is fearful; what will be the result of all this? Candide, on the other hand, has perfect justifications for the deaths. Note also the fates of the victims. Both men were similar in morals and actions; if anything, the Inquisitor was the more corrupt. But he is buried with the full honors of a Cardinal in a church, while the Jew, being an infidel, is thrown on the dungheap.

CHAPTER TEN: DESCRIBING THE DISTRESSING CIRCUMSTANCES IN WHICH CANDIDE, CUNEGONDE, AND THE OLD WOMAN REACHED CADIZ, AND HOW THEY SET SAIL FOR THE NEW WORLD

Cunegonde was robbed of her jewels, and bewailed her fate; where would she find more Jews and Inquisitors to replace them? The old woman suspected a friar who stayed with them the night of the theft. Candide, quoting Pangloss, said that since worldly goods are common to all men, everyone has the right to take them. It would have been nice, however, if the friar had left them with enough money to finish their journey. In response to his question, Cunegonde says that they do not have a farthing. The old woman suggests that they sell one of the horses, and that she ride behind Cunegonde (although it will be difficult, since she has only one buttock).

The horse was sold to a Benedictine prior for a few pesetas. The three then continued their journey, and at long last reached Cadiz. The fleet was at Cadiz, being provisioned for a trip to Paraguay, where they were to put down a group of Jesuits and Indians. These people were inciting tribes to revolt against the Kings of Spain and Portugal, and had to be taught a lesson. Candide showed his skill at drilling to the General, and was so impressive that he was made a captain of infantry in the little army. And so the fortunes of the three travellers, once so low, reached a high point.

The trip to Paraguay was filled by many arguments centering around Pangloss' philosophy. Candide hopes that all will go well in the New World; he admits that some bad things had happened in Spain and Portugal. Cunegonde shudders at the things she has seen and experienced. Cunegonde is calmed by Candide, who notes that the waters are calmer and the winds less variable than in Europe; surely this is a good omen. Still, she admits to having lost almost all hope. The old woman interrupts this dialogue: if they had had the misfortunes she experienced, they would not complain. Cunegonde thought it amusing for the old woman to pretend to have had unfortunate experiences. Calling her by name for the first time (Abigail), Cunegonde recounts her experiences, and asks how the old woman can rival them, especially as the younger woman is a baron's daughter and has never served as a kitchen maid.

Abigail replies that Cunegonde knows nothing of her birth, and that if she would be shown her buttock, Cunegonde might suspend her judgement. This intrigued the young people, and they listened to Abigail's story.

Comment

This is another transitional chapter, one which takes the action from one area to the next. It also serves to introduce Abigail's story, which is told in the following chapter. Thus, there is little to interest us here. Once again, Voltaire shows his anti-clerical sentiments by having a friar steal Cunegonde's jewels. Candide escapes from Cadiz through his military knowledge; he could have left by no other means. One interesting note is Candide's reaction to the loss of the jewels. He says that since all goods belong to all men, perhaps the friar had the right to take them-a **satire** of Rousseau's philosophy. Candide also remarks that it would have been nice if the friar had left enough money for them to continue their travels. In the next few chapters, Voltaire will mount a strong attack against Rousseau, especially that philosopher's "Noble Savage" thesis.

CHAPTER ELEVEN: THE OLD WOMAN'S STORY

The old woman was not always so ugly and worn. She was the daughter of Pope Urban X and the Princess of Palestrina. (In a footnote, Voltaire notes that there has been no Pope Urban X and praises the author for not ascribing a bastard to an actual Pope, showing his tenderness. Of course, Voltaire indicates by this footnote that it was quite common for Popes to have bastards.)

Until she was fourteen, the old woman lived in grand palaces and had all she could want. By that time she was already the object of desires. She had beautiful breasts and eyes. Poets praised her eyes, and dressing maids fell back in astonishment at the beauty of her body.

Abigail had been betrothed to the Prince of Massa-Carrara, her equal in beauty, charm and grace. They loved each other dearly. The marriage was planned, and was to have been celebrated with great pomp. The whole of Italy seemed engaged in preparing for the great day. Just before the wedding, however, the Prince's former mistress invited him to have a drink of chocolate with her. He died less than two hours later in horrible convulsions.

The intended bride and her mother were naturally distressed by this event, and they decided to leave their home for a while and travel to an estate the mother owned near Gaeta. But again their plans were altered; their yacht was attacked by Moorish pirates. "Our soldiers defended themselves like the Pope's guard: they fell on their knees and threw away their arms, begging the pirates for absolution at the point of death."

The soldiers were stripped naked, as were all the ladies aboard the yacht. Then the Moors proceeded to search one and all. "What surprised me more was that they put their fingers into a place where we women normally admit nothing but a syringe tube. This seemed to me an unusual custom, but that is how we regard everything new when we first leave our native country." Abigail soon learned that the pirates were searching for diamonds, which women often hide in such places and remarked parenthetically that the Maltese Knights of St. John follow the same procedures; it is an established point of international law.

The women were taken to Morocco on a slave ship, and they suffered many indignities. All were attacked regularly. "I was ravishingly lovely, the pattern of beauty and grace; and I was a virgin-but not for long." The pirate captain, "an odious negro," tore her virginity from her, and considered that he was doing her a favor.

Morocco was bloody at the time of their arrival. The fifty sons of Emperor Muley Ismael were fighting to take power, and there were fifty wars going on at once. The pirates were subdued by a rival faction soon after they disembarked, and the gold and women were carried off. The old woman notes that people who live in the tropics have hotter blood and desires, than those to the north. They fought like lions over the money and the women. "A Moor seized my mother by the right arm, and my captain's lieutenant held her by the left; a Moroccan soldier took her by one leg, while one of our pirates clung to the tower." Similar things happened to all the other women. The captain tried to hide Abigail behind him, and defend her with his sword. She saw all the other women torn limb from limb by the sailors. Soon all were either dead or dying, in one large heap. Such events were quite common at the time. "Yet they will not miss one of the five daily prayers prescribed by Mahomet."

The old woman freed herself from the pile of corpses and crawled to the shade of a large orange tree. There she collapsed and fell asleep, overcome by exhaustion. She was awakened by a good looking European, who muttered words of appreciation at her beauty while standing over her almost dead body.

Comment

There are several interesting points-besides those dealing with the Pope's illegitimate children-in this chapter. Voltaire agrees with Rousseau in the belief that Locke's tabular rasa theory is valid; at birth, all are without prejudices and other devices held by culture and civilization. But where Rousseau is hopeful, Voltaire is cynical about the future of man. All civilizations are corrupt; all contain cruel and irrational institutions. In this chapter, and several which follow, Voltaire pokes fun at non-European societies. We shall see, for example, the bloody civilizations of the Americas. Rousseau calls the Indians "Noble Savages." Voltaire considers them more savage than noble. In this section, he alludes to the Moslem civilization. Some writers of the Enlightenment considered Islam a superior religion and civilization than Christianity and the West. Islam had a tradition of culture and learning at a time when Europe was in the "Dark Ages," and Islam was more tolerant of religious differences than the Europe of the Reformation period and after. Yet, we find in this chapter a description of a bloody battle, which did not prevent the Moslems from their five prayers a day. Like the Christians, then, the Moslems are faithful to the forms of religion, but often ignore the content.

CHAPTER TWELVE: THE OLD WOMAN'S MISFORTUNES CONTINUED

Abigail was delighted to hear her native language. She told the man of her misadventures, and then fell into a swoon. He carried her to a nearby house, where he put her to bed, gave her something to eat, and then left her to sleep. Later on he waited on her with great care and told her that she was the most beautiful person he had ever seen, regretting that he could not restore her virginity to her.

The man was born at Naples, where they castrate two thousand boys a year. (During this period, musical pieces were written for the castrato voice. Castratos were children who were castrated to prevent them from attaining puberty, at which time their voices would change. Thus, a boy soprano might become a tenor or baritone. A castrated boy soprano would become a castrato.) Some of the children died, some attained great fame with their beautiful voices; others became prime ministers. This man had had a successful operation; he was organist to the Princess of Palestrina.

Abigail was overcome. The Princess of Palestrina was her mother! She tells her protector this, and he is amazed. He had been her teacher, and even then she showed promise of beauty. You are right, says Abigail, and her mother is in that pile of corpses not far from here. The woman then told her protector of her experiences, and he told of his. He had been sent to the King of Morocco by a Christian prince as part of a trade for gunpowder and other war materials, which would enable the prince to destroy other Christian princes. Now the protector (a castrated person is called a eunuch) is finished with his mission, and is about to return to Italy. He offers to take the woman home with him.

The woman was overcome with gratitude, and thanked her protector. But instead of returning her to Italy, he sold her to the Governor of Algiers. Soon after, a plague broke out in the province, and spread over three continents. (The old woman asks Cunegonde what she knows of plagues. Cunegonde replies that she knows nothing of such things. The old woman says that plagues are far worse than earthquakes, and that she caught it.) Thus, a well-brought up bastard of the Pope had yet another misfortune added to her young life! She did not die, however, but the eunuch, the Governor, and almost the entire harem perished.

When the first effects of the plague passed, the Governor's slaves were sold. A trader purchased her, and took her to Tunis.

There she was sold to another trader, who took her to Tripoli, where she was again sold. Then to Alexandria, to Smyrna, and to Constantinople, each time being sold to another trader. In the end she belonged to a captain of the Sultan's guard, who went to Azov to fight the Russians.

The captain took his harem with him, housing the women in a fortress near the Sea of Azov. The Russians attacked, destroyed the city, and set siege to the fortress, hoping to starve the inhabitants into submission. The soldiers guarding the harem swore never to surrender, but soon ate the eunuchs. Then they decided to eat the women.

A Moslem priest delivered a sermon of life to the soldiers. "Do not kill the women," he said. "Instead, cut one buttock from each lady, and eat that. Then, you may cut other pieces if the siege lasts. Allah will be pleased at such a charitable action, and the siege will be relieved." The soldiers agreed, and that is how the old woman lost one of her buttocks.

Soon after the Turks had finished their meal, the Russians overcame the fortress, and killed every soldier. The Russians ignored the women, many of whom were near death. But French surgeons are everywhere; one of them was found, and he saved many of the women's lives. He assured the ladies that such practices as cutting off buttocks were quite common, and in accord with the laws of warfare.

As soon as the women could walk, they were sent to Moscow. Abigail was sold to a noble, who made her his gardener and whipped her twenty times a day. Two days later he was broken at the wheel for court intrigues, and she escaped. She made her way across Russia and then across Europe, growing old in the process (with only half a behind). But she never forgot that she was a daughter of the Pope, and was in love with life. "This ridiculous weakness is perhaps one of our most melancholy propensities; for is there anything more stupid than to be eager to go on carrying a burden which one would gladly throw away, to loathe one's very being and yet hold it fast, to fondle the snake that devours us until it has eaten our hearts away?"

The old woman met many who hate their lives, but only twelve of these committed suicide. She ended by becoming a servant in Don Issacher's house. Now she is waiting woman to Cunegonde. She would not have told her story if not asked. The old woman tells Cunegonde that it would be amusing to persuade each passenger on the ship to tell his or her story, "and if you find even one who has not often cursed his life and told himself that he is the most miserable man alive, you can throw me into the sea head first."

Comment

Despite its appearance, *Candide* is a serious work by a bitter man who sees the stupidities of his world, and has the wit to unmask them. Voltaire makes us laugh, but at the same time recognize the inconsistencies and stupidities of his times, and our own. There is little **satire** in this chapter, with the exception of the priest's suggestion for the cutting off of buttocks instead of complete cannibalism. Here we have the hypocrisy of Eastern religion, which is as bad as that of the West. Later on, the old woman is assured that such treatment is in accord with the laws of warfare. Thus, this barbaric practice is sanctified by the Church and State alike. Of course, all of this is gross exaggeration, the method by which Voltaire points out the foibles of societies. Yet, it is and was true that the civil and religious authorities condone many barbaric practices. This is the only important piece of

satire in the chapter. Allowing for minor exaggerations, the old woman's story might almost be true. Thus, Voltaire presents a stark picture of his society and adds, at the end, that the old woman's story is not unusual; everyone on the boat could tell similar tales. Such are the irrationalities we must face that all of us, at one time or another, wish to give up our lives out of despair, despite the fact that life is our greatest possession.

CHAPTER THIRTEEN: HOW CANDIDE WAS FORCED TO LEAVE THE LOVELY CUNEGONDE AND THE OLD WOMAN

After having heard the old woman's story, Cunegonde paid her the respect due a person of her rank. She also asked the other passengers to tell of their adventures. After hearing them, she admitted that the old woman was right. Candide wished Pangloss had not died, for the philosopher would undoubtedly have had some observations to make on the matter.

At long last, the ship reached Buenos Aires. The three travellers went to see Governor Don Fernando d'Ibaraa y Figueora y Mascarenes y Lampourdos y Souza, who was (obviously) a nobleman. The Governor was most arrogant. He also had a greed for women, and was immediately taken by Cunegonde. He asked whether she were the captain's wife or sister. This alarmed Candide, who was confused as to the answer. She was not his wife, but on the other hand she was not his sister, and he could not claim that she was. In addition, Candide was too pure to make up a white lie. So Candide replied that Cunegonde would soon become his wife, and he asked the Governor to attend the wedding.

The Governor smiled, and told Candide to review his troops. While our hero was gone, the Governor declared his love for Cunegonde, and swore to marry her the following day. Cunegonde asked for time to collect her thoughts. She then asked the old woman for advice. The old woman advised her to marry the Governor; for she may have a coat of arms, but hasn't a farthing to her name. Besides, why should Cunegonde defend her fidelity, especially after her sexual escapades of the past few years. The old woman said that if she were Cunegonde, she would marry the Governor without a moment's hesitation. While they talked, a ship entered the harbor, with a group of secret police and a Spanish magistrate aboard.

The old woman was correct when she guessed that the friar had stolen Cunegonde's jewels at Badajoz. The friar tried to sell the jewels to a jeweler, who on recognizing them as belonging to the Inquisitor, turned the friar over to the Inquisition. Before being hanged, the friar confessed that he had stolen the jewels from Cunegonde, and described the three travellers. The Spanish officials on the ship had been sent to find and punish them. The old woman, on realizing what had happened, saw what was to be done. She drew Cunegonde aside, and told her she had nothing to fear since it was Candide who had killed the Inquisitor; the Inquisition was not after her. Besides, the Governor lover her and would not allow her to be molested in any way. The old woman then spoke to Candide, advising him to flee so as to avoid being burned at the stake. Cunegonde had to be abandoned once again. Where would Candide find shelter?

Comment

The Governor's long name implies Voltaire's distaste for the pomp and falseness of the nobility of his period. The old woman, after having gone through many ordeals, advises Cunegonde to be an opportunist, and look out for herself. One wonders what Pangloss would have said at such a moment; he was the idealist as opposed to the old woman, a realist. The old woman advises Candide to flee. This will save him from certain death, and also remove an annoying person from the path she has chosen for Cunegonde.

CHAPTER FOURTEEN: THE RECEPTION CANDIDE AND CACAMBO MET WITH FROM THE JESUITS OF PARAGUAY

It seems that there was a fourth member of the band which fled from Cadiz: a servant of the type often found in Spain and the colonies. This servant, Cacambo, had mixed blood and had served in a variety of jobs. Cacambo was devoted to Candide, and on hearing the old woman's advice, immediately saddled two thoroughbreds. He urged Candide to leave while the coast was clear. Candide burst into tears at the suggestion. He was sorry to leave Cunegonde, especially since the Governor had agreed to come to their wedding. And what would happen to Cunegonde now? Cacambo assured him that all would be well.

"Women are never at a loss. God looks over them." Candide asks his servant where they were going. Cacambo replies that they had been going to make war on the Jesuits before this turn in their fortunes had taken place. Now that things were changed, they would instead fight on the side of the Jesuits. He is certain the Jesuits will be delighted to have a trained military man like Candide on their side. "When you don't get what you want on one side, you find it on the other." Candide asks Cacambo if he had been to Paraguay before. The servant replies that he had once been in the employ of the College of Assumption, and knows the land well. He explains that the Jesuits have a wonderful system. They own the entire land and the people own nothing: this is a masterpiece of reason and justice. The Jesuits are most godlike. They fight the Kings of Spain and Portugal in Paraguay, and absolve them of sins in Europe. In Paraguay they kill Spaniards, and in Madrid they bless them.

The two set out on their journey. At the first frontier post, Cacambo tells the guard that a captain wishes to speak with the Jesuits. News of their arrival is sent to the city. Candide and Cacambo are disarmed and dismounted, and taken to the Jesuit colonel. The colonel makes a sign, and the two men are surrounded by soldiers. They are told they must wait; only the Father Provincial is allowed to speak to Spaniards, and he gives them only three hours to stay in the country. Cacambo asks the whereabouts of the Father Provincial, and is told that he has said mass, and is now on parade. The visitors will not be able to kiss his spurs for another three hours. Cacambo tells the soldier that Candide is not a Spaniard, but a German, and is hungry. Can't they have something to eat while they wait? The colonel is told of this, and agrees to speak with Candide.

Candide is taken to a beautiful arbor, and is served a meal on gold dishes; the Paraguayans eat corn on wooden dishes in the open fields.

The colonel was a handsome young man with a proud look on his face. Before sitting down, Candide kissed the hem of the colonel's cassock. The colonel spoke in German, asking Candide if he were a German. Candide replied that he was. The colonel (a Jesuit as well), asked Candide what part of Germany he was from. Candide (perhaps assuming the colonel hated Germans) replied that he came from "that dirty province of Westphalia," and the castle at Thunder-ten-tronckh. This amazes the colonel. He asks if it really can be Candide. Both men are astonished, and embrace. The Jesuit colonel is none other than Cunegonde's brother, who all had thought dead! How happy Pangloss would have been to have seen this.

The colonel dismisses the servants, and embraces Candide again, giving thanks to God all the while. Candide tells the colonel that Cunegonde is still alive. The colonel asks, where, and Candide tells him that she is with the Governor at Buenos Aires. He admits that he had come to Paraguay to make war on the Jesuits. The two men continue their meal, while waiting for the Father Provincial. Meanwhile, the colonel tells Candide his story.

Comment

Note how easily Candide changes sides in the war. Cacambo, like the old woman, is a realist, and tells his master that it doesn't really matter which side you fight on in a war; fight for the side which offers you the most. This is Voltaire's comment on the meaning of war, and an answer to those who fought for holy causes. Voltaire was born in the aftermath of the wars of the Reformation, which divided Europe in two, and later into still more camps. Millions were killed, and Voltaire, studying the history of the period, concluded that it was not worth a single death. His strong anti-clerical feelings can be traced in part to this. Note too his discussion of the differences in position taken by the Jesuits in Europe and Paraguay. The Jesuits were a contentious group at the time *Candide* was written; because of their maneuverings, they were finally expelled from France and other countries in Europe. Voltaire shows their duplicity and cunning. Such maneuverings may be permissible in a political organization, but are they to be condoned in a religious order? Voltaire considered the Catholic Church more a political than religious organization, and wrote of it as such. In this chapter we have another example of Voltaire's reintroducing a character because it suits his purposes. This time it is Cunegonde's brother; other examples will follow.

CANDIDE

TEXTUAL ANALYSIS

CHAPTERS 15 - 19

CHAPTER FIFTEEN: HOW CANDIDE KILLED THE BROTHER OF HIS BELOVED CUNEGONDE

Cunegonde's brother tells Candide what has happened to him since they last met. He will never forget the day the Bulgars came to the castle. After they had left, he and others believed to be dead were taken to be buried in a Jesuit chapel. A Jesuit sprinkled holy water on the bodies, and some of it got into the brother's eyes. The Jesuit noticed his eyelids flicker, examined the body, found it to be alive, and rescued him.

Cunegonde's brother, the colonel, was handsome, and the reverend father took a fancy to him. He became a novice, and then was sent to Rome where some German Jesuit recruits were needed. It seems that the rulers of Paraguay prefer non-Spanish Jesuits, whom they consider not as shrewd as the Spanish type. Thus, the brother was sent to Paraguay, and quickly rose to the position of colonel. He is sure his forces will be able to defeat those of Spain, and is glad that Candide will help them. The two embrace, and the colonel promises Candide they will ride in triumph through the town and rescue Cunegonde. Candide hopes so, for he still expects to marry her. The colonel is angered by this; Candide lacks the breeding to marry his sister. Candide is dumbfounded at this outburst. He had rescued Cunegonde from all sorts of difficulties, she is under his obligation, and in addition, wants to marry him. Pangloss had told him all men are equal, and he believes it.

The colonel does not accept this, and strikes Candide across the face with the flat of his sword. Candide then draws his own sword and kills the colonel. He is immediately overcome with grief; he has killed his former master, friend, and future brother-in-law. Candide has killed three men, and two of them were priests. And he is a mild mannered man!

Cacambo hears the scuffle, and rushes in. Candide tells him that all they can do is get ready to die like heroes with swords in their hands. But Cacambo has been in such scrapes before, and he keeps his head. He undresses the colonel, and tells Candide to put on his clothes, which he does. Then Cacambo tells him to mount a horse and ride out of the place as quickly as possible. Everyone will think he is a Jesuit messenger. To spur his master on, Cacambo runs in front of the horse, telling all to make way for the reverend father colonel.

Comment

The brother is saved from burial by the sprinkling of holy water. A religious person might have called this a miracle, but the brother, an opportunist, does not comment on his good fortune, only saying that the holy water was "disgusting stuff." He then says that he joined the Jesuits because a reverend father took a fancy to him. There is an implication here of homosexuality; the Jesuits and other orders were continually being accused of sexual irregularities. Voltaire does not go into this matter; in a work noted for its unusually broad **satire**, this line is almost thrown away, a fact which leads many to believe that the author had no intention of exploring or even raising the matter. The colonel strongly opposes his sister's marriage to Candide, primarily because of Candide's lack of lineage. So much for the equality of Christian men!

CHAPTER SIXTEEN: THE ADVENTURES OF TWO TRAVELERS WITH TWO GIRLS AND TWO MONKEYS, AND WHAT HAPPENED TO THEM AMONG THE SAVAGE OREILLONS

Candide and Cacambo crossed the frontier before the colonel's body was discovered. Cacambo had taken enough provisions for the trip, and so they had no fear of starvation. They plunged ahead into unexplored lands, which had no roads. They finally came across a lovely meadow, and Cacambo suggested they stop to eat. How can he eat, asks Candide, when he has just killed the Baron's son, and will never see Cunegonde again? What is the use of living? What will the Jesuits' magazines say?

While talking, Candide ate heartily. As the sun set, the two travellers heard what sounded like women's voices. They ran to see what it was, and found two naked girls running along the edge of the meadow, while two monkeys ran after them, nibbling at their buttocks. Candide was touched at the sight, and so picked up his double-barreled rifle and killed the monkeys.

Candide tells Cacambo he is overjoyed. He has delivered the two girls from danger, and so has made amends for having killed the Inquisitor and the Jesuit. He suspects the two girls are of noble birth. They may prove useful in their journeys.

As Candide spoke, the two girls embraced the dead monkeys and began to cry. Candide admires their magnanimity, but Cacambo realizes that they are really distraught; Candide has killed their lovers. Candide cannot believe this. He charges that Cacambo is laughing at him. How can the monkeys be their lovers? The servant asks why Candide is surprised by everything. In some parts of the world monkeys are the lovers of humans. They are partly human, after all, just as he is partly Spanish. Candide admits that Cacambo may be right. Pangloss had spoken of such unions, which took place in the old days, and produced fauns, centaurs, and satyrs. He admits, however, that he never believed these stories. Cacambo replies that such disbeliefs are the result of a faulty education. He adds that he now fears the girls will play some trick on them.

Candide agreed, and he and Cacambo cautiously left the meadow and took shelter in the woods. After dinner and a round of cursing their enemies, they went to sleep. When they awoke they found that during the night they had been tied to a tree by the Oreillons, the natives of the country. It seems that the two girls had told the Oreillons that they were there. Now they were surrounded by fifty naked, and armed savages. Some were heating a large caldron. Others were screaming that their captives were Jesuits. The savages seemed overjoyed; they would have Jesuit for dinner (apparently a great delicacy).

Cacambo was afraid the girls would play a trick on them because of the monkey's deaths, and repeats his warning to Candide. Candide sadly says that they will either be roasted or boiled. What would Pangloss say about this? No doubt all will turn out for the best, but it was sad to have lost Cunegonde and be eaten by the Oreillons. But Cacambo hasn't given up yet; he knows Oreillon language, and will speak to the savages. Candide tells the servant that he should make them understand "how outrageously inhuman it is to cook their fellow-men, and that it's scarcely the act of a Christian."

Cacambo speaks to the savages. He asks them if they are looking forward to eating a Jesuit for dinner. He has no objection to such a meal; it is correct to treat your enemy in such a manner. The law of nature itself teaches us to kill our fellow-creatures. If we don't eat them afterwards, it's only because we have something else to eat. The savages don't have the same resources as the Europeans, and so it makes more sense to eat Jesuits than leave the bodies to crows and ravens. But he and Candide are not Jesuits. Candide is the great enemy of the Jesuits, and they are about to kill and eat him! And further, he, Cacambo, was born in this country! Candide, on his part, has just killed a Jesuit and has carried off the spoils. If the Oreillons do not believe this, they can take Candide's gown to the nearest frontier post of the Jesuits, and find out to whom it belonged. This will not take much time, and if he is not telling the truth, then he can still be eaten for dinner; "you are too well acquainted with the principles and customs of international law not to use us courteously."

The Oreillons were impressed with this argument, and sent two of their number to the frontier with the gown. When they returned they verified Cacambo's story, and both master and servant were released. Indeed, they were treated royally, being offered girls, refreshments, and other such things. Then they took the two to the border of their land, shouting. "He was never a Jesuit! Not he!"

Candide admired the Oreillons. What a fine bunch of fellows they were! What culture! If he hadn't been lucky enough to have killed Cunegonde's brother he would surely have been eaten. There is certainly a lot to be said for the goodness of unsophisticated nature.

Comment

In this chapter, Voltaire deals with the nature of education and Rousseau's Noble Savage. Being a European, Candide is shocked when he sees the girls and the monkeys, and even more shocked when he learns that the monkeys are the lovers of the girls. Thus, there are many different civilizations, each with its own sometimes peculiar values and cultures. The author picks a particularly unusual example to demonstrate his point, perhaps pointing out that many European customs are equally ridiculous. Then our heroes are captured by the Oreillons - Rousseau's Noble Savages - who plan to eat them. Again, Voltaire demonstrates they are more savage than noble. They think that Candide is a Jesuit, and since they hate the Jesuits but apparently consider roast Jesuit a delicacy, they prepare to eat him. All is changed when they discover that he is one of them; he has killed Jesuits also. Thus, Voltaire warns his readers what to expect if they follow Rousseaus' advice and live among the Noble Savages. Such people are no better than the Europeans- but on the other hand, they are no worse. Cacambo tells us that the only reason Europeans do not eat those they kill is because they have a more plentiful larder. Thus, why go to the Americans to live among the Noble Savages, when their types can be found in Europe? Observe also that after being freed, Candide praises the savages; they have not eaten him, because he killed a Jesuit. This is contrasted to the previous chapter, when he says that he is doomed because he has killed two men of God; here he rejoices in having killed the Jesuit, an act which has saved his life. This change in attitude implies that Pangloss was right: all turns out for the best in this best of all possible worlds.

CHAPTER SEVENTEEN: HOW CANDIDE AND HIS SERVANT REACHED THE COUNTRY OF ELDORADO AND WHAT THEY SAW THERE

Cacambo spoke to Candide when they reached the Oreillon frontier. Since the new world is no better than the old, he said, why not return to Europe? How shall we get there, asks Candide, and where shall we go when we arrive? His own country is full of Bulgars and Abars, cutting each other's throats. He will be burned alive if he returns to Portugal, and skewered if he remains in Paraguay. And how can he leave without Cunegonde? Cacambo does not answer these questions, instead suggesting that they head for Cayenne. Perhaps the Frenchmen of the city can help them, and maybe God will have pity on them.

The two travellers had a difficult time on their journey to Cayenne. They met many obstacles, both natural and human. Their horses died of fatigue, and their provisions were exhausted. Finally Cacambo admitted that they could go no further. Seeing an empty boat by the side of a nearby river, he suggested that they fill it with coconuts, board it, and then drift down the river. Even if they did not find something good, they could not be in worse shape than they were at the time. Candide agreed, and the two boarded the ship and trusted in Providence.

The stream took them several miles, and then broadened into a river. The river disappeared into a cave, evoking fear in the two passengers. They drifted into daylight in twenty-four hours, and soon after the boat was dashed to pieces on some boulders.

The travellers had to crawl along the river bank for three miles. Finally they reached an open plain surrounded by mountains. Everything was quite beautiful; there were many people, all of whom seemed rich and handsome. The carriages were drawn by large red sheep which were faster than the best horses. Candide remarked that the land seemed better than Westphalia, and he led the way into a nearby village.

On the outskirts of town, they saw some children wearing tattered gold brocade playing ninepins. The pins and balls were colorful, and when Candide picked them up to examine them, he found that they were made of gold, emeralds, and rubies. He immediately assumed the children were the sons of the King of the country. When a teacher appeared, he thought he was the tutor of the Royal Family.

The children dropped their toys and ran away. Candide picked up the precious playthings and handed them to the tutor, making a deep bow, and observing that Their Royal Highnesses had forgotten their nuggets and precious stones. The schoolmaster merely smiled and walked away. Candide and Cacambo continued on their way, picking up many rubies, emeralds, and large gold nuggets as they went. Candide wondered what land they were in. He assumed the King's children must be well-mannered if they were taught to despise gold and precious stones. Even Cacambo was surprised at this, and said nothing.

The travellers approached a palatial house. Many people were standing around, and delightful music could be heard. The smell of cooking wafted through the door. When Cacambo approached the entrance he heard Peruvian spoken. This was his native language, and he offered to act as Candide's interpreter.

The house turned out to be an inn, and the travellers entered, and were invited to take seats. Wonderful dishes were placed before them, including a two-hundred pound boiled vulture. The plates were of rock crystal, and all were wonderfully rich. The travellers held polite conversations with some of the guests, and all was most pleasant.

When the meal was over, Candide and Cacambo tried to pay with two large gold nuggets. On seeing the nuggets, the innkeeper and his wife laughed loud and long. When they recovered, the innkeeper spoke. He told the travellers that they were not used to strangers in their country, and begged to be excused for laughing at them. He assumed that Candide had no money, but told him that none was needed. The inns were maintained by the government, and open for the convenience of tradespeople. He apologized for the poorness of the meal, but promised that they would be treated better in the larger cities.

The travellers were amazed at all this. This was surely the strangest country in the world! All must go well here. "And whatever Professor Pangloss might say," noted Candide, "I often noticed that all went badly in Westphalia."

Comment

This chapter serves as an introduction to one of the most important sections of the book: the one which deals with the magical Kingdom of Eldorado. The Kingdom is not magical in the sense that it contains sorcerers or the like, but rather because it is a land of reason: the ideal land discussed by many Enlightenment philosophers. Carl Becker, in his book on Enlightenment philosophers entitled The Heavenly City of the Eighteenth-Century Philosophers, notes that the thinkers of this period were medieval in the sense that they, like St. Thomas and others, believed in perfection being possible. If man would but use his reason, he could plan and execute perfect forms of government. Examples of this approach are to be found in Montesquieu's *Spirit of the Laws* and Rousseau's *The Social Contract*. The two works are dissimilar in their philosophies and the solutions they offer for the world's ills, but alike in their belief that perfection is attainable here and now, through the use of reason and the destruction of irrational elements of life which are, in reality, vestiges of an imperfect age. This, then, is the background for the introduction of Eldorado in *Candide*. Voltaire heightens the effect by having the travellers arrive in the country after a series of unusual journeys. This makes the transition from Paraguay, and the land of the Oreillons, all the more striking in the contrast. Now he places Candide, the man of the Enlightenment, into the Heavenly City of the philosophers. The last words in the chapter lead us to believe that Candide accepts it as such; he notes that despite all Pangloss said about Westphalia, it was not a good place to be. We will now see how he reacts to the land of perfection, and find out what Voltaire thinks of man's nature and his ability to cope with things rationally.

CHAPTER EIGHTEEN: WHAT THEY SAW IN THE COUNTRY OF ELDORADO

As befits its importance, this is the longest chapter in the book. It deals with the society of the perfect kingdom, its customs and traditions, its values, and finally, the reaction of a typical European to the life of reason, once it is presented to him in real rather than abstract terms.

Cacambo is curious about the land of Eldorado, and engages the innkeeper in conversation. But all the innkeeper would say was that he was an ignorant fellow, and knew nothing. He does say that there is an old man in the neighborhood, the most learned person in the land, who can answer all their questions. The innkeeper then takes the two travellers to the old man, who lived in a modest silver home paneled in gold, with a hall encrusted with rubies and emeralds.

The old man was seated on a couch stuffed with hummingbird feathers. He greeted the two, and after offering them refreshments, they began to talk. The old man told them that he is 172 years old. The Kingdom in which they find themselves used to be inhabited by the Incas, who left it to fight elsewhere. A few remained, and they founded the present nation. They passed a law that no one could leave the Kingdom, in this way hoping to preserve its innocence and happiness. The Spaniards had some knowledge of the Kingdom, and called it Eldorado. Sir Walter Raleigh almost reached it at one time. But the nation is protected by natural barriers from Europeans, whose only desire is to take the pebbles and dirt found in the soil, and would gladly kill for such trifles.

After a while, Candide inquired about the religion of the country, asking whether one existed. The old man said that the people were surely religious; they have a strong sense of gratitude for what they had. Candide again asks what the religion was. The old man replies with a question: "Can there be two religions, then? I have always believed that we hold the religion of all mankind. We worship God from morning to night." Cacambo asks if the people worship only one God, and the old man answers that of course they do. Then Candide asks how the people pray. The old man responds that the people never pray. "We have nothing to ask of God, since He has given us everything we need. But we thank him unceasingly." The travellers then ask to see the priests. The old man smiles and says that all people are priests, but the King and the head of each family perform rites every morning, thanking God for the blessings they have received. Candide is puzzled; are there no monks to dispute, govern, and intrigue? The old man cannot understand this; in fact, he doesn't know what a monk is. Candide is delighted with this. If Pangloss were alive, he would admit that Castle Thunder-ten-tronckh is not the loveliest place on earth.

When the conversation ended, the old man ordered a carriage to take the travellers to Court, and bade them fond farewell. Candide and Cacambo entered the carriage, and it took them to the Court in less than four hours. The Court was beautiful, being constructed of an unknown material superior to gold. Twenty lovely maidservants greeted them, and helped them dress in garments made of hummingbird down. Then they were conducted to the main chamber. Cacambo asked one of the lords there whether he should grovel before the King or lick the dust off the floor when he arrived. He is told that the custom is to embrace the King and kiss him. Thus, Candide and Cacambo embrace the King when he arrives.

Since there is time before supper, the travellers are shown the sights of the Court. Candide asks to see law courts, and is told there are none; in fact, court cases are unknown. Further, there are no prisons. He was shown a long and impressive Palace of Science, however.

Afterwards, Candide and Cacambo had supper with the King and his companions. The conversation was most witty, with Cacambo acting as translator for the King and Candide.

The travellers spent a month at Court. Every day Candide spoke of the wonders of the place. Still, he said, he could never be completely happy without Cunegonde; if Cacambo were in love, he would understand this better. He then thinks of the meaning of Eldorado. While in that Kingdom they are like everyone else. But what if they loaded twelve sheep with the precious stones, and took them back to Europe. Then they would be the richest people on the continent. They would have nothing to fear from the Inquisition, and would be able to rescue Cunegonde.

Cacambo was glad to hear this. He was restless, and had had enough of Eldorado. Like Candide, he was anxious to take riches back to Europe and boast of what they had seen and done. So they decided they were no longer happy, and asked to leave the Kingdom.

The King thinks their plan is foolish. He realizes that Eldorado is a modest place, but it works well enough to please most people. On the other hand, he has no right to detain strangers.

"All men are free." The two may go when they wish, but they will find the journey difficult and dangerous. He promises to have his engineers construct a machine to take them out of Eldorado in comfort. They will be guided to the frontier by his subjects, but then must find the way out by themselves; citizens of Eldorado are not allowed to cross the border. The King then promises to provide the two with anything they wish. Cacambo asks for a few sheep loaded with stones and mud (precious gems and gold dust). The King laughs; he cannot understand why Europeans love mud and stones, but they can take all they wish. The engineers are then ordered to make a machine for transporting the two travellers. Three thousand scientists worked on it, and it was completed in fifteen days. Candide and Cacambo were placed in the machine, together with two large red sheep which they were to ride after crossing the mountains. In addition, they were provided with twenty sheep loaded with food and thirty to carry presents. Fifty additional sheep carried the gold and precious stones. The King embraced Candide and Cacambo, and wished them good luck. The guides then took them to the frontier. Candide was delighted. If Cunegonde were being held for ransom by the Governor of Buenos Aires, they now had more than enough money to pay it. He told Cacambo that they would go to Cayenne and set sail from there. Then they would see which kingdom they would buy.

Comment

A good part of this chapter is concerned with the religion of Eldorado. Although the old man does not call it Deism, that is what it is. The citizens of Eldorado believe in God and give thanks for their blessings, but there is no organized priesthood, and no rigid theology. Without these, there can be no bigotry or religious wars. As for monks, whom Voltaire obviously dislikes even more than priests, the old man doesn't even know what they are. It is clear that toleration is ever-present in Eldorado; the citizens of this land have no reason to hate one another, to kill, or to persecute others for their beliefs or possessions. Thus, there are no law courts or jails. All are equal; the King is embraced, and not groveled before as is the case in Europe. Note that in the same paragraph in which Voltaire states there are no law courts or prisons in Eldorado, he mentions the Palace of Science. Perhaps he hopes to indicate here that with the rise of science, crimes will disappear, and law courts will become obsolete. With all this, Candide is delighted. Yet, he is not happy: two desires impel him to leave Eldorado. He still loves Cunegonde, and will not be happy without her. In addition, he would like to take the gold and precious stones to Europe and make a name for himself in his old country. Cacambo, who lacks a sweetheart, agrees with Candide that it would be better to be rich in Europe than like everyone else in Eldorado. Note that Candide is not happy in a land where all men are reasonable. This is Voltaire's way of saying that man searches for the heavenly city, but once he finds it, rejects it for the life of irrationality. This is his response to the perfection-seekers of the eighteenth century. The reader might note that a modern novel, Lost Horizon by James Hilton, seems to be based on this same idea. In this story the hero comes across a magical land-Shangri-la-and he too leaves it to return to the irrational world outside the high mountains.

CHAPTER NINETEEN: WHAT HAPPENED TO THEM AT SURINAM, AND HOW CANDIDE MADE THE ACQUAINTANCE OF MARTIN

The travellers spent the first day of their journey to Cayenne happily, thinking of their great wealth. But on the second day two of the sheep plunged into a bog, and other misfortunes followed. After a hundred days, only two sheep were left. Candide reflected on these misfortunes, and told Cacambo that the riches of the world are perishable. The only solid things in life were virtue and the prospect of seeing Cunegonde. Cacambo was more optimistic; they still had a great deal of treasure, and he believed that the Dutch city of Surinam was over the horizon.

As the travellers approached the town, they noticed a Negro lying across the road, wearing nothing but a pair of blue canvas drawers, and lacking a left leg and right hand. They asked him what he was doing there. The Negro responded that he worked for Mr. Vanderdendur, the owner of a famous sugar-works. Candide then asked if he was treated badly by his master. The Negro replied that it was customary to treat people such as he in that manner. He received one pair of canvas drawers a year.

Those who catch their fingers in the grindstone while working at the factory have a hand chopped off. Those who try to escape lose a leg. "That's the price of your eating sugar in Europe." The Negro says that his mother sold him in to slavery on the coast of Guiana for fifty shillings. Before she left him, she said: "Always honor and adore your fetishes, my dear boy, and they will make you happy; you will have the honor of being a slave for milords the white men, and that is how you will make your parents' fortune." The slave says that he doesn't know whether their fortune was made by the sale, but he is certainly miserable. Even the animals are better off than the slaves. The slaves was told by those converted him to Christianity that all men are children of Adam. This men as that his master is his cousin. Why should relatives treat him so badly? Candide is shaken at this. What would Pangloss say about such a situation? The slave's pessimism seems more valid than Pangloss' optimism, and Candide fears he must cease being optimistic. Cacambo asks the meaning of the term "optimism." Candide replies that "it's the passion for maintaining that all is right when all goes wrong with us." Candide turns toward Surinam, his eyes filled with tears.

On arriving at the city, the travellers ask whether a ship will leave soon for Buenos Aires. They agree to meet a Spanish captain at an inn, and they take the two sheep with them. Candide tells their story to the captain, including his desire to rescue Cunegonde. The captain refuses to take him to Buenos Aires, for Cunegonde has become the Governor's favorite mistress, and he would kill anyone who tried to take her away. Candide weeps at this. He then turns to Cacambo, and tells him to take some of their five or six million diamonds to Buenos Aires, and offer the Governor a million of them if he frees Cunegonde. If he should refuse, Cacambo is to raise the offer to two million. Cacambo hasn't killed an Inquisitor, so he shouldn't have much difficulty.

Meanwhile, Candide will go to Venice, a free state where he will be safe. Cacambo agrees that the plan was a good one. The two embraced, and before parting, Candide told his servant not to forget to take care of the old woman as well as his beloved Cunegonde.

Candide waited a while in Surinam after Cacambo's farewell. He tried to find a ship to take him to Venice, and while he looked, he purchased provisions for the journey. At last he met Mr. Vanderdendur, who in addition to owning the sugar-works was the owner of a large ship. Candide asked him for the price of a journey to Venice. The ship captain suggested ten thousand piastres, a price which Candide quickly accepted. But Mr. Vanderdendur, seeing Candide's quickness, realized that he must be quite rich. He then said that the trip could not be undertaken for less than twenty thousand piastres. Again, Candide was quick to agree. Then Mr. Vanderdendur raised the price to thirty thousand; again Candide said he would pay the sum. Mr. Vanderdendur then realized that the two sheep must be loaded with great wealth, but decided not to raise the price again, and instead wait and see what happened. Candide sold to small diamonds, and received more than thirty thousand piastres for them. He gave the money to Mr. Vanderdendur, and prepared to sail. The captain made certain that the sheep were loaded on board before Candide arrived. He then set sail without our hero. Candide turned back to the shore, aware that he had lost a tremendous fortune.

Candide decided to lay the matter before a Dutch judge. The judge fined him ten thousand piastres for having knocked too loudly on the door, an additional ten thousand for costs, and then promised to look into the matter when the captain returned. All of this drove Candide to distraction, and he was plunged into a deep melancholy. But he continued his search for a passage to Europe. At last he found a ship about to leave for Bordeaux. Having lost his fortune, he took a modest berth. To objectify his dissatisfaction, he offered to pay the passage of any honest man, and give him an additional two thousand piastres, if that man was dissatisfied with the province, was the most unfortunate man there, and wanted to leave. There were many candidates, so to make his task easier, Candide chose some twenty who looked sociable. They then went to the inn, where Candide heard their stories. The winner would receive the passage and the money, while the others would be given consolation prizes. Candide then listened to the stories until four o'clock in the morning. As he listened, he remembered the old woman's conversation with Cunegonde, when she challenged Cunegonde to find a single person who had not suffered misfortunes. He then thought of Pangloss, and considered how puzzled the philosopher would have been about all this.

Candide decided to award the prize to a poor scholar, who had lost his family, been robbed and persecuted, and in other ways had suffered reverses all his life. The other candidates were as unfortunate as the scholar, but Candide awarded him the prize in the hope that he would relieve the boredom of the long journey. The other candidates then declared that Candide was doing them still another injustice. Candide mollified them by giving each one hundred piastres.

Comment

The problems of Surinam seem striking when contrasted with the glories of Eldorado. The first person to greet the travellers is a Negro slave who tells his sad story. In this way, Voltaire contrasts the real world with the Heavenly City. To further heighten the comparison, he notes that this is the price

Europeans must pay for their sugar and luxuries: human misery. Then Candide is cheated by a captain, and when he seeks a travelling companion, hears other sad stories. All of this makes him doubt the optimism taught by Pangloss. Note the cynical definition of optimism he gives Cacambo when the servant asks the meaning of the word.

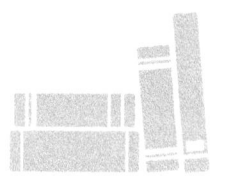

CANDIDE

TEXTUAL ANALYSIS

CHAPTERS 20 - 24

CHAPTER TWENTY: WHAT HAPPENED TO CANDIDE AND MARTIN AT SEA

Candide, along with the poor scholar-whose name was Martin-boarded the ship and set sail for Bordeaux. During the long voyage, they occupied themselves discussing moral and physical evils. But there was a difference between these two unfortunate souls: Candide dreamed of Cunegonde, while Martin looked forward to nothing. In addition, Candide still had some gold and diamonds left from his almost completely lost fortune. Remembering this, Candide returned to the philosophy espoused by Dr. Pangloss.

The scholar was asked by Candide what he thought of the problem of evil. Martin replied that the clergy of Surinam accused him of denying the divinity of Christ. He believes that man was created by evil forces, and not good ones. Candide does not believe this, but Martin repeats his assertion. If you look about you, he says, you will see the work of the devil everywhere; God must have deserted the planet, with the exception of Eldorado. Every town wants the destruction of nearby towns; families wish to destroy other families; "the weak detest the strong and cringe before them, and the strong treat them like so many sheep to be sold for their meat and wool." Europe is full of assassins, who range the continent from one end to the other committing murder and mayhem. Concluding his speech, Martin says that he is forced by experience and observation to believe that man's origin is evil. Candide insists that there must be some good in the world. There may be, says Martin, but he hasn't seen any.

While they were talking the sound of gunfire reached the ship. Two warships were fighting, some three miles away. The ships approached, and Candide could see the men fighting, and a hundred poor souls dying on the deck of one of the ships, which was about to sink. They were swallowed by the sea soon after. Martin then tells Candide that this is a prime example of what he had been taking about. Candide admits that something is diabolical about all this. As he spoke, he saw a bright red object in the sea. It was one of his sheep! Candide was overjoyed at finding him, especially since he was still loaded with riches.

The captain soon discovered that one of the ships had been a Dutch vessel, and the other, Spanish. The sunken ship had been the very one commanded by the man who had cheated Candide! Our hero turned to Martin, and observed that crime is sometimes punished, the captain got what he deserved. But Martin noted that the passengers, who were without fault, were also lost at sea. God punished the scoundrel, but the devil drowned the rest. This conversation continued for a long while, and although it got no further, the two men enjoyed it. Candide was content; he petted sheep, and said that now that he had found it, he would surely find Cunegonde soon as well.

Comment

In this chapter Voltaire discusses the question of good and evil in a brief, but telling manner. The argument is familiar: If God is all good and all powerful, how does one explain the existence of evil? Martin, whose life has been filled with tragedies, has the answer: God is not all powerful at the present time, although he might have been a long while ago. The world is controlled by the devil, and it is he who is responsible for the evil and suffering in the world. In one of the most powerful passages in the book, Martin describes the state of Europe, and asks how one could explain this in terms of an all-powerful, all-benevolent God. Candide thinks he has his answer when the sheep is returned to him, and the evil captain is punished by drowning. But Martin notes that a hundred or so innocent people died in the same disaster. Thus, if God punished one evil man, the devil punished a hundred innocent ones. Although Voltaire does not say so, he seems to imply here that the devil may be a hundred times more powerful than God. But Candide, after questioning Pangloss' philosophy in the previous chapters, seems to have returned to the optimism of the earlier part of the book. He has his sheep and his money, and believes he will soon find Cunegonde. The troubles of the past seem behind him; his good motives in saving Martin from his fate in Surinam are now submerged, as his optimism blinds him to the fate of his fellow men. From the time he lost the sheep to the time he saw one of them swimming in the sea, he was concerned with the fate of mankind. During this time, he questioned Pangloss' philosophy and became a pessimist to all intents and purposes. The periods in which he is optimistic about the future, he tends to ignore his fellow men. Is Voltaire saying that the optimist is less human and humane than the pessimist? This seems to be the case.

CHAPTER TWENTY-ONE: WHAT CANDIDE AND MARTIN DISCUSSED AS THEY APPROACHED THE COAST OF FRANCE

At last the coast of France was sighted. Candide asks Martin whether he has ever been to this country. Martin responds that he knows France well: the three major occupations of the people are love, backbiting, and talking nonsense. Paris is chaotic, full of people searching for pleasure without finding it. When he was there last he was robbed by a pickpocket, and then jailed for eight days on suspicion of being a pickpocket himself. Later on the became a printer's reader, so as to earn enough money to return to Holland.

Candide is not eager to see France. "You will appreciate that after spending a month in Eldorado, a man is not interested in seeing anything except Lady Cunegonde." He will wait for her in Venice, and must cross France to Italy. Candide then asks Martin to accompany him on his voyage, and Martin agrees to do so. It is said that Venice is no place for the poor. Since Candide is not poor, he will be happy to follow him there.

Candide then changes the subject. Does Martin believe that the earth was originally part of the sea? He has read this in a book the captain had. Martin replies that he doesn't believe it any more than anything else he reads in books. But why was the world created, asks Candide. To drive us mad, says companion. Then Candide asks Martin if the story of the two Oreillon girls who loved the monkeys astonished him. Martin says that he was not surprised. He has seen so many strange things, that nothing surprises him. Candide asks Martin if he believes man has always been as wicked and depraved as he is at the present time. "Do you think that hawks have always eaten pigeons when they could find them?" was the answer. Candide believes they always have. Then, says Martin, if hawks have not changed their character, why does Candide suppose that man is any different today than he was yesterday? Candide begins his answer, which involves the fact that man has free will, when he hears that the ship has reached Bordeaux.

Comment

Voltaire cannot ignore the opportunity to criticize his countrymen in this chapter, in which the travellers arrive in France. The French are silly people, who are often wicked. Paris is a most depraved city. Yet, the shortness of the chapter, and the rapidity with which Voltaire changes the subject, leads us to question the depth of this criticism. True, he had sharp words for his adversaries, and always praised Britain to the detriment of France, but there was a residue of nationalism in the man. After discussing France, Candide engages in a conversation about sundry matters with his companion. Martin proves to be a skeptic of the first order. Nothing surprises him, he says. What he really means is that he has encountered nothing but evil in his lifetime, and is no longer surprised by the cruelties of the world. One suspects that he would be amazed by goodness, that is, if he could recognize it as such. Man is evil, he says, and was always evil. Candide's response is begun when the ship reaches Bordeaux. He was about to argue that man may change, since he has free will. To this, Martin might have said that man has never used this free will for good, and why expect him to do so in the future? Martin speaks for Voltaire in this section, and reflects the author's contempt for the efforts of some of his contemporaries to reform the world.

CHAPTER TWENTY-TWO WHAT HAPPENED TO CANDIDE AND MARTIN IN FRANCE

The travellers' experiences in France occupy most of this, one of the longest chapters in the book.

Candide purchased a carriage in Bordeaux, and prepared to travel to Venice. He regretted leaving the sheep behind, but gave it to the Academy of Sciences, which then established an annual prize for an essay on the topic: "Why are Sheep's Fleece Red?" The prize was won by a scholar who proved, through the use of mathematics, that sheep were necessarily red and should die of scabs.

Candide discovered that everyone he met along the road was going to Paris. He decided to make a side trip to that city. He entered the city, which was as bad as the filthiest city in Westphalia. On reaching his hotel, he was overcome by a slight sickness. Since he wore a large diamond ring and had a great cash box, he was soon attended by two doctors he had not sent for, some friends who would not leave him, and some ladies who tried to feed him hot broth. Martin observed that he was also ill during his first trip to Paris. No one attended him, and so he recovered.

Candide's friends soon succeeded in bringing him to the brink of death with their care and medicines. A priest was called in to administer last rites. He asked Candide for a promissory note payable to the bearer in the next world. Candide refused to enter into such an agreement. His new lady-friends said it was all right; it was a new custom. Candide still refused, since he was not a man of fashion. Martin was angry, and threatened to throw the priest out the window. The priest retaliated, by threatening not to bury Candide. Martin replied that he would bury the priest unless he left. After some more arguing, Martin threw the priest out the front door. The priest was offended, and initiated a law suit.

Candide recovered, and while he convalesced, had some people of fashion to supper. These people played cards for high stakes, and Candide joined them. Candide was surprised to find that he never drew an ace; Martin was not a bit surprised.

A spry abbe from Perigord showed Candide around town. He was a fawning type, who knew all the gossip and joined in the most expensive entertainments. The party went to the theatre to see a new tragedy. Candide wept through the performance, although a group of critics nearby made snide comments. One of them spoke to Candide during the intermission: Candide was wrong to weep; it was a bad play, acted by bad performers. He offered to bring Candide twenty hostile reviews of the work the next day. Candide turned to the abbe, and asked how many plays have been written in French. Five or six thousand, is the answer. Candide says "That's a lot," and then asks how many are good. The abbe replies that fifteen or sixteen are good. Candide repeats his first comment: "That's a lot."

Candide enjoyed the performance of the actress who played the part of Queen Elizabeth; she reminded him of Cunegonde. After he told the abbe that he would like to pay his respects to her, the abbe offered to introduce the two at his house. This troubled Candide. How are Queens of England treated in France? He was raised in Germany, and matters of etiquette trouble him. The abbe replied that they are treated with respect while still beautiful, but after death are thrown on the dunghill. This shocked Candide, but Martin assured him that the abbe was correct; that is what happened to Minimia, who was thrown on the dungheap after death. Candide thought this was highly improper behavior. Martin, always the skeptic and cynic, replied that such is what one learns to expect in this life. "Imagine every possible contradiction and inconsistency, and you will find them in the government, the law-courts, the churches, and the whole life of this absurd nation."

Candide then notes that the people of Paris always seem to be laughing. Why is this so? The abbe replies that they laugh at odd times, such as during the commission of horrible crimes. (Obviously, then, since they are always laughing, they are always doing something horrible.) What of the men who laughed during the performance of the tragedy? They are evil-minded people, answers the abbe. They are critics, who enjoy damning every play and book. "He hates a successful writer, just as eunuchs hate successful lovers. He is one of those snakes of literature who feed on dirt and venom. He's a pamphleteer." Candide asks what sort of work a pamphleteer does. The abbe replies that a pamphleteer deals in odd sheets of paper; he is a journalist. While they spoke, the crowd left the theatre.

Candide swears that he is eager to see Cunegonde, but he would also like to have supper with the actress (Mademoiselle Clairon), whose acting he so admires. But Clairon moves in the best circles, and the abbe (contrary to what he said before) did not know her friends. Still, he has a suggestion; he will introduce Candide to a lady of quality who will give him four years of experience of Parisian life. Candide is curious, and goes to call on the lady.

The lady and a group of twelve friends were busy playing cards when Candide, Martin, and the abbe arrived. The lady was seated near a banker, watching with care the progress of the game. This care was not idle curiosity; she was making certain the players did not mark the cards. The lady was aided by her fifteen year old daughter, who also watched the game avidly. Indeed, they were so intent on their task that they didn't notice the entry of the three men. Candide was surprised by this, and noted that the Baroness of Thunder-ten-tronckh had better manners. But just then the abbe whispered something in the lady's ear, and she rose to greet Candide. It seems that she was a Marchioness with a passion for gaming. Candide was then shown a seat, handed a pack of cards, and invited to join the game. He lost fifty thousand francs in two deals.

After the game the group went to dinner. All were surprised by the fact that Candide did not seem bothered by his heavy losses. The footmen though he must be an English lord.

The group had a typical Parisian supper: there was much noise, many witticisms (some good, most bad), a little politics, and a great deal of slander. They discussed some new books. The abbe asked if the group had read a book by Gauchat. One of the guests said he had, and like so many works of the time, it was pointless; he found much more enjoyment at cards. And what of Canon T.'s essays? Another guest thought they were boring. Then the talk turned to tragedies. A guest asked why some tragedies were acted when they were unreadable. A man of taste replied that sometimes a play could interest an audience although it might have little merit. Dramatists must have fresh ideas, but they must not be fantastic. They must be sublime, yet neutral. They must be poets yet none of their characters may be poets. They must know the language, but must not allow the **rhyme** to dictate the meaning. Those who break the rules may write a successful play or two, but will never be great writers. There are very few good tragedies.

These words impressed Candide, who was seated next to the Marchioness. He asked her who the man of taste was.

She replied that he was a scholar, who didn't play cards but sometimes came with the abbe and stayed for supper. He had written unsuccessful plays and novels. Candide thought he was a great man, perhaps another Pangloss. He turned to speak to the author. Did he believe that all was for the best in this world, and could not be otherwise? The author replied that he did not: all is wrong with the world, and no one knows his place. Life is a perpetual civil war. Candide thought he had seen worse, and spoke of Pangloss, who believed that there might be shadows in the most beautiful picture. Martin interrupted, saying that the shadows were in reality horrible blemishes. Candide agreed, but said that the blemishes are man-made, and man could not do otherwise. Martin accepted this, saying it was not their fault.

Most of the guests could not follow this conversation, and continued their drinking. Candide told some of his life-story to the Marchioness. After dinner she led him to her room, and sat him on a couch. She asked if he were still devoted to Cunegonde, and Candide replied that he was. The Marchioness smiled, and said that he spoke like a Westphalian; a Frenchman would have admitted love for Cunegonde, but would have added that he loved her more. Candide was agreeable to this: "Very well, Madam, I will answer as you wish." The Marchioness continued, saying that Candide began to love Cunegonde the moment he picked up her handkerchief. She then asked Candide to pick up her garter. Candide did so. The Marchioness was expansive: sometimes she let her would-be lovers wait for weeks, but she would surrender to Candide that night, as a courtesy to the visitor from Westphalia. She then praised Candide's two diamonds, which he wore on his hands. Soon after she was in possession of them.

Afterwards, Candide felt remorse at having been unfaithful to Cunegonde. The abbe sensed Candide's remorse, and suited himself to the mood. It seems that Candide had lost fifty thousand francs at cards in addition to the two small diamonds. The abbe hoped to cultivate Candide, and profit thereby. And so he talked with him of Cunegonde. The abbe said that Cunegonde must be witty, and her letters charming. Candide admitted that he had no letters from her. He told of Cacambo's voyage, and of his waiting for an answer from the servant. The abbe thought about this for a moment, and then left.

Candide received a letter, apparently from Cunegonde, the next day. In it she said she was ill, that she had left Cacambo and the old woman behind but that they would soon follow, and that the Governor of Buenos Aires took all the riches. She closed with the wish that Candide join her as soon as possible. Candide was overjoyed; he drove with Martin to the address given in the letter, and rushed into the house, and then into the bedroom. A figure was in the bed. Candide shouted Cunegonde's name, but a nurse told him to be still, and that Cunegonde could not speak. But a hand emerged from the bed. Candide, believing it to be Cunegonde's, covered it with diamonds and then placed a bag of gold on an armchair in the room. As all this was happening, the abbe arrived with some officers. One officer asked the abbe whether Candide and Martin were the suspicious strangers he had told them about. The abbe said they were, and the officers seized the two men. Candide protested: "This is not the way travellers are treated in Eldorado." Martin said that he was more convinced than ever of man's essential evil. Candide asked where they were to be taken, and was told they would be placed in a dungeon.

At this point, Martin realized that the lady in the bed and the abbe were both frauds. Did this mean the officers were frauds as well? Perhaps they could be gotten rid of easily. Martin spoke with Candide, and our hero showed the officers three small diamonds. The officers were touched. All strangers were placed under arrest, they said, but Candide had nothing to fear. One of the officers had a brother near Dieppe. If given a diamond or so, he would take care of him. Candide asked why all strangers were arrested. The abbe replied that a beggar heard some people talking nonsense, and soon after committed murder. This was not a murder of the fashion of May, 1610 (here Voltaire refers to the assassination of King Henry IV), but rather after the fashion of December, 1594 (the crowning of Henry IV). Candide is puzzled. This land frightens him. He asks the officer to take him to Venice, where he will once again see Cunegonde. But the officer can only take him to lower Normandy. With this, the handcuffs are removed from Candide and Martin, and the two are taken to Dieppe. For the price of three diamonds a boatsman takes them to Portsmouth, England. Although this was not the way to Venice, Candide was happy; at least he was delivered from the hell of France! He would start out for Venice at the first opportunity.

Comment

This chapter is a commentary on France, the Church, and the cupidity of mankind. It begins, however, with Candide donating his sheep to the Academy of Sciences, which immediately sets up an essay contest on the question, "Why are Sheep's Fleece Red?" It is won by a mathematical fool. This is an obvious reference to the many similar essay contests held by the magazines edited by the philosophes. Rousseau first came to prominence with the writing of one such essay. This essay, the Discourse on the Sciences and Arts (1750) was criticized by Voltaire, and the author may here be lampooning Rousseau and those who follow him. With this out of the way, Candide and Martin go to Paris, which Voltaire describes as a filthy city. The Parisians are evil people who laugh at the misfortunes of others. The clergy are even worse. One tries to sell Candide an indulgence, and the seemingly friendly abbe is out to rob Candide of his wealth. Doctors do not fare any better; the doctors are as venal as the clergy; when they hear the rich Candide is ill, they come running, without having been asked. Candide almost dies under their treatment. Then Voltaire turns to the press, and more particularly, to critics. These men cannot write themselves, and so spend their lives criticizing those who do. So much for them! And what do they expect? If there are fifteen good plays out of the thousands written, says Candide, that's still quite a lot. At the dinner party, Candide meets a man of taste who sets forth seemingly intelligent rules for the writing of plays. Candide is quite impressed, even though he later discovers that the man cannot write himself. Thus, Voltaire indicates that those who claim there are rules for writing are knaves or fools.

CHAPTER TWENTY-THREE: CANDIDE AND MARTIN REACH THE COAST OF ENGLAND, AND WHAT THEY SEE THERE

While travelling to England, Candide and Martin discuss their problems. Candide asks Martin what he makes of the world; his friend finds it "a senseless and detestable piece of work." Candide changes the subject, and asks Martin if he knows England. Are they as mad there as in France? Martin replies that they are, but in a different way. The two nations are fighting, and spending huge sums, for control of Canada, a snowy, worthless place. The English are different from the French, however: they are serious and gloomy.

The ship reached Portsmouth, and Candide noticed a crowd watching a stout man, who was kneeling, with his eyes bandaged, on the deck of a warship. Four soldiers fired shots into his skull, and everyone seemed happy. Candide asks the meaning of this performance, and is told that the stout man was an admiral who did not have enough dead men to his credit. He engaged in battle with a French ship, and did not come close enough alongside. Candide noted that the French admiral was as far from the English ship as the English admiral was from the French ship. That is true, answered an onlooker, but in England, it seems to pay to shoot an admiral from time to time.

All this shocks Candide, and he refuses to set foot on English soil. He goes to bargain with the captain, who agrees to take the ship to Venice after being promised more money. After a long voyage, the ship was safely anchored at that city. Candide is overjoyed; at last he will see Cunegonde. He is now on the right road, and the outlook seems fine; his old optimism returns in full force. He seems sure that Cunegonde will be there, for he has great trust in Cacambo.

Comment

The only purpose for this chapter is to allow Voltaire to make an observation about the English. He sees no sense in the imperial wars France and England fought throughout the eighteenth century, and says so. He believes the English to be a gloomy race, but does not follow this up with examples. The reader will remember that the observations of the French in the previous chapter were buttressed by many stories in which their unsavory practices were exposed. This is not the case here. Instead, Voltaire limits himself to the story of the execution of the admiral, and then whisks Candide to Venice. It is almost as though he changed his mind about the nature of the chapter after having begun it. Voltaire admired the English over all other people in Europe, and yet spends only a few hundred words on that nation. Perhaps this can be explained by the fact that *Candide* was written hurriedly; it is not the polished, finished work which Voltaire usually published. Thus, there are gaps, contradictions, and the like, as well as the type of misproportion discussed here. In a way this is to be expected; the story of *Candide,* while interesting and informative, is not the purpose of the book. The work is a philosophical tract and work of criticism set in the form of a novel. This helps explain the curious nature of this chapter and others.

CHAPTER TWENTY-FOUR: ABOUT PACQUETTE AND BROTHER GIROFLEE

As soon as the travellers set foot on land, they began their search for Cacambo. Although they looked everywhere, he was not to be found. Every ship arriving in the port was examined, but still no Cacambo. Candide is disturbed by this. He has spent a good deal of time in his journey to Venice. Surely Cacambo and Cunegonde should have arrived there before him. He can only conclude that Cunegonde is dead, and if is so, he might as well die also. How much better it would have been to remain in Eldorado instead of returning to Europe. Martin is right: "there is nothing here but illusion and one calamity after another." Candide then sank into a deep depression, and nothing could rouse him from it.

Martin remains the cynic. Candide is surely a simple person, to believe that a mongrel servant with five or six million in his pocket would follow his directions. If Cacambo found Cunegonde, he probably took her for himself; if he didn't, he would find another wench. Martin advises Candide to forget his sweetheart and his servant. These words offer Candide no consolation; he became more melancholy, as Martin proved that all the world was horrible, with the exception of Eldorado, and no one could go there.

One day, while the two were discussing the matter, Candide noticed a young monk walking arm in arm with a girl. As they walked, the girl looked lovingly at the monk, and from time to time pinched his cheeks. Candide observed that these two seemed happy, and offered to bet Martin that they were most content. Martin accepted the bet. Candide suggested that they invite the two to dinner, and then they would see who was right and who was wrong. Candide approached the pair, and invited them to a sumptuous feast. The girl blushed, but the monk accepted at once. As they walked to the inn, the girl glanced at Candide in astonishment and confusion, and she begun to cry. Once in the room, she spoke to Candide. Didn't he recognize Pacquette? Candide was astonished: this was the girl who had gotten Pangloss in all that trouble at the castle! Pacquette admits that she is the one, and then settled down to tell Candide her story.

She has heard of Cunegonde's horrible experiences and those of others, but says that her life has been worse. When they first met, she was an innocent girl, and so her confessor had little difficulty in seducing her. Then horrible things happened. She was forced to leave the castle soon after Candide was ejected. If a famous doctor had not taken pity on her, she might have died. But she became the doctor's mistress, and for a while was content. Then the doctor's wife became jealous, and started to beat her every day. The doctor was a most ugly man, and Pacquette did not love him. Imagine being beaten for a man you don't love! It is dangerous, however, for a cross woman to marry a doctor. She fell ill, and he gave her some medicine; within two hours she was dead. Then her relatives pursued the doctor, who was forced to flee. Pacquette was put into prison, and her innocence would not have saved her were it not for the fact that she was pretty. The judge released her, on condition that she become his mistress. All seemed well, but shortly thereafter the judge got a new mistress and threw her out of his house. Pacquette had no choice: she became a streetwalker. She fondled businessmen, lawyers, monks, gondoliers, and abbes. And with no prospect of either earthly or heavenly rewards! She is one of the unhappiest persons alive.

When she ended, Martin turned triumphantly to Candide, and claimed to have won half the bet. Candide was puzzled; Pacquette seemed so happy in the street, fondling the monk and pinching his cheeks. That's the way things are, she sighed. Yesterday she had been robbed and beaten by an officer, and today she must seem happy to please a monk. Candide then admitted that Martin was right, and the four sat down to dinner.

During the meal, Candide spoke with the monk, whose name was Brother Giroflee. He said that the monk was a lucky fellow. He is healthy, has a pretty girl, and seems happy with his place in the Church. The Brother says this is not so; he has often considered burning the monastery to the ground, and becoming a Turk. His parents sent him to the monastery in order to leave more money to an older brother, whom he curses. The monastery is filled with quarrelsome, jealous men. Some of his sermons bring him money, but the Prior robs him of half of his take. However, he does have enough left for his girls.

Martin again turns to Candide, and claims to have won the bet. Candide agrees, and pays him two thousand piastres. He also gives Brother Giroflee one thousand piastres, telling Martin that it will make them happy. Martin disagrees: the money will make them more unhappy. Candide changes the subject, and observes that a man often runs into people he never expected to see again.

Perhaps he will meet Cunegonde in Venice. Martin hopes she will make Candide happy one day, but he doubts it. Candide calls Martin a pessimist, but Martin replies that he is what life has made him. Look at the gondoliers, says Candide. See how happy they are, singing all the time. But Martin observes that they are probably not so happy at home with their wives and children. What of the senator, Pococurante, asks Candide. He lives in a beautiful palace, and is said to be most happy. Martin replies that he would like to see him. Candide then asks permission to see Pococurante.

Comment

The core of this chapter is Pacquette's story. Here Voltaire takes the opportunity to attack the highest elements of European society using the device of a streetwalker. In his masterpiece, In Praise of Folly, Erasmus does much the same thing. Pacquette was seduced by her confessor, and then roughly used by people who make up the cream of the professions. Brother Giroflee, a corrupt monk, is not an evil man per se; he simply has no vocation, and was placed in the monastery for family considerations. His monastery is not a place of quiet contemplation, but rather of constant bickering. Thus, says Voltaire, even basically good, or banal men, may be corrupted by the corrupt institutions of the Europe of his day.

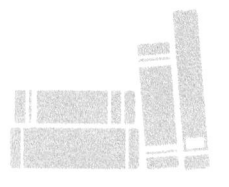

CANDIDE

TEXTUAL ANALYSIS

CHAPTERS 25 - 30

CHAPTER TWENTY-FIVE: A VISIT TO COUNT POCOCURANTE, A NOBLE VENETIAN

Candide and Martin visit Pococurante the next day. The senator greeted them cordially, but coldly: Candide was unnerved, but Martin (perhaps because he expected nothing) was pleased. They are served by two pretty girls. Pococurante says that he sometimes sleeps with them, as the ladies of the town annoy him. But the two serving-girls are becoming a bore, and he may get rid of them soon.

After they finish their refreshments, Pococurante takes them for a walk along his gallery, where they are shown beautiful paintings, some by Raphael. But these give the senator no pleasure; he no longer looks at them. Then, before dinner, they hear some music. Candide thinks it beautiful, but it only bores Pococurante. They argue a little, but discreetly. For his part, Martin agrees with the senator.

The three have an excellent dinner, and afterwards retire to the library. Candide looks at the books, and spies a finely bound copy of Homer. He compliments Pococurante on his taste; Pangloss used to say that it was a most excellent book, and Pangloss was the most famous German philosopher, Pococurante doesn't particularly care for Homer-he bores him to distraction. He has found that the endless succession of battles and gods bore many learned men. Does the senator feel the same about Virgil? Pococurante likes parts of the Aeneid, but this too doesn't interest him greatly. He prefers Tasso and Ariosto. Then does the senator like Horace? Pococurante launches into a learned disquisition on Horace, but ends with disapproval. "I read only to please myself, and enjoy only what suits my taste."

This astonishes Candide, who had been raised never to rely upon his own judgement. Martin agreed with everything Pococurante had to say. Candide then asks the senator his opinion of Cicero. His host has never read his works; Cicero is always in doubt about everything. "I decided that I knew as much as he and needed no one's help to remain ignorant." Martin asks Pococurante about the eighty volumes of the proceedings of the Scientific Academy which line the walls. There must be interesting items in those works. There might be, says the senator, if the authors had devoted their time to useful pursuits, like the making of pins. As it is, they wrote of vain philosophical systems "devoid of any useful information." But what of all the fine plays, asks Candide? The senator says that he has three thousands of them, and not three dozen are any good. His collection of sermons is utterly useless, and no one has ever opened any of his books on theology, including himself.

Martin turns to a shelf full of English books. He believes that many of these will appeal to the senator, who is, after all, a republican. Pococurante agrees that it is a great privilege to write what one thinks; the English do this. Italians never do this. "Those who live in the country of the Caesars and the Antonines dare not entertain an idea without the permission of a cleric. But the same liberty which inspires the English leads to the corruption of factions, which tends to destroy liberty." Then Candide notices a volume of Milton's works, and asks Pococurante's opinion of that author. He is told that Milton is a barbarian, who distorts the meaning of the Book of Genesis, who has spoiled Tasso's conception of Hell and the Devil, does not understand the humor of Ariosto, and in other ways proves his inferiority. It was despised by the English when first published, and Pococurante agrees with this assessment. All of this distresses Candide, who admires Milton and Homer. He whispers to Martin that their host probably has a low opinion of German poets as well. Martin sees no harm in this. But Candide believes Pococurante is a genius; nothing pleases him.

The senator then takes his guests into his garden. Candide admires its beauty, but Pococurante will only say that it is not displeasing. He plans to revamp the garden the following day.

After taking leave of Pococurante, Candide tells Martin that the senator is the happiest man alive; he is superior to all he possesses. But Martin does not accept this: Pococurante is disgusted with everything he has. But, says Candide, there is pleasure in criticizing all and uncovering faults where others see beauty. Are you saying, asks Martin, that there is pleasure in not being pleased? Candide does not answer, but again changes the subject: he will be happy when he sees Cunegonde again. Martin is dubious, but says there is no harm in hoping. His pessimism seems well-founded, as Cacambo does not appear after more weeks of waiting.

Comment

This chapter is dominated by Pococurante, the jaded, intellectual, and sometimes cynical nobleman. At times, the senator resembles Voltaire himself. His opinions of Homer and Milton are those of the author, and Voltaire's opinions can be found in other parts of the chapter. This may best be seen in the senator's opinion of the English. After slighting the English in the previous chapter, he alludes to them in the scene in the senator's library. Pococurante admires the English, but warns of the dangers of extreme freedom in politics; so did Voltaire on many occasions. After leaving the senator, Candide and Martin discuss him; this is Voltaire looking at himself, and revealing himself to the reader. Is he really happy? Martin thinks not, for what joy is there in criticizing all. Voltaire calls for high standards, and does not find them. This does not mean that he is happy; on the contrary, he is one of the saddest of men, for he sees the world more clearly than others.

CHAPTER TWENTY-SIX: HOW CANDIDE AND MARTIN SUPPED WITH SIX STRANGERS, AND WHO THEY WERE

One evening, while Candide and Martin had supper with some strangers at the inn, they were approached by a dark man, who grabbed our hero by the arm. He told Candide to be ready to leave with him. Candide looked up, and immediately recognized Cacambo. He was overjoyed to see him; "surely Cunegonde is here too," he thought. He demanded to be taken to her at once, so that they could die of joy together. Cacambo said that Cunegonde was not in Venice, but in Constantinople. Candide was surprised, but undaunted: he would go to his beloved even if she were in China. He tells Cacambo he wishes to leave for Constantinople at once. Cacambo replied that they can leave after supper. He adds that he is a slave, and his master is waiting for him.

Candide was delighted with the news, but saddened to learn that Cacambo was a slave. Still, he sat with Martin and others till the meal was over. Cacambo served one of the guests, and when he was finished, approached him and said that "Your Majesty can leave when you wish. The gondola is ready." He then left the room. The other guests, who were there for a carnival, were astonished. Then another servant approached and said "Sire, Your Majesty's carriage is at Padua, and the boat is ready." The master nodded, and the servant left. The remaining guests seemed puzzled. Then a third valet approached a third guest, and similar messages were given. The same thing happened with the fourth and fifth guests. Candide and Martin thought that all were characters taking part in a carnival masquerade. But then a sixth servant approached the sixth guest, and said that he had no more credit; he feared they both would be in jail before long, and was taking his leave.

After all the servants disappeared, Candide spoke to the six guests. Could it be that all were kings? Cacambo's master spoke first, telling Candide that he was Grand Sultan for several years, only to be dethroned. His nephew, the new Grand Sultan, has allowed him to go to Venice for the carnival. The second guest turned out to be the former Emperor Ivan of Russia; he too had come for the carnival. The third was Charles Edward, King of England, who was dethroned for brutality; he is on his way to Rome to visit his father, who was also a dethroned monarch. The fourth, a dethroned King of Poland, was in Venice for the carnival. The fifth was also a former King of Poland, but he was fortunate enough to become King of the Sarmatians; he was in Venice for the same reason as the others. Then the sixth monarch spoke. Although not of noble birth, he was once King of Corsica. Once rich and powerful, he now has nothing. But he, too, has come to Venice for the carnival.

The five kings were touched, and gave money to the sixth. On his part, Candide gave him a large diamond. The others were surprised; who was this wealthy commoner? They rose from the table and prepared to leave. As they did, four more former kings arrived, wishing to see the remainder of the carnival. But Candide did not notice them; he thought only of Cunegonde and Constantinople.

Comment

In this short chapter, Voltaire tells us that Cunegonde is in Constantinople, and so sets the scene for Candide's next journey. In addition, he tells the story of the six kings. There is not much complexity to this tale; Voltaire merely tries to show that a member of royalty is just like other men and is humanly subject to good and bad fortune. Thus, he dismisses the concept of divine rights.

CHAPTER TWENTY-SEVEN: CANDIDE'S JOURNEY TO CONSTANTINOPLE

Cacambo interceded for Candide with the Turkish captain who was to take his master back to Constantinople. And so Candide and Martin embarked for that city and Cunegonde. While on their way to the ship, Candide remarked on the wonder of their dinner with the six kings. He, a commoner, has been able to help a monarch! Perhaps there are other monarchs as unfortunate as the one they met. Candide considers himself lucky (as he does whenever things turn for the better; at heart, he is always the disciple of Pangloss); all he has lost is a number of sheep. Thus, he concludes, Pangloss was right. Martin is not so sure; all he can say is "I hope so."

Once aboard ship, Candide found Cacambo and spoke with him. How is Cunegonde? Is she still as beautiful as ever? Did Cacambo buy her a palace at Constantinople? Cacambo replies that Cunegonde has become an old, ugly slave, who washes dishes for an old Prince, who himself is a refugee. Candide takes the news quite well. Whether Cunegonde is beautiful or ugly, he is still an honest man, and will love her always. But how did Cacambo lose all the money? The servant showed impatience. He had to give the Governor of Buenos Aires two million to take Cunegonde away from that city. The rest was stolen by a pirate, who forced him to become a slave. Candide is sorry for Cacambo, and reflects that he still has enough money to purchase Cunegonde's freedom, and how sad it is that she is now ugly. But he is no longer sure that he is so fortunate. He asks Martin whether he is any better off than some of the deposed kings. Martin answers that he cannot know until he looks into their hearts. Candide thinks that Pangloss would be able to answer the question if he were there. Martin is dubious; what scales would the philosopher use to measure misery? As for him, he thinks there are millions of men with more to complain about than the kings. This is possible, says Candide, whose optimism has been shaken by his conversation with Cacambo.

Eventually the ship reached Constantinople, and Candide bought Cacambo's freedom. Then he set off to look for Cunegonde. Among the galley slaves on his ship were two very poor rowers. Candide took an interest in them, and noticed at once that they resembled Pangloss and Cunegonde's brother. He spoke of this resemblance to Cacambo, and the slaves overheard the conversation. They dropped their oars in amazement, an act which led the captain to whip them with gusto. Candide begged him to stop, and offered to buy the slaves. The slaves looked at him, and said "Good Heavens! It's Candide!" It seems that Candide was not mistaken. The two slaves were indeed Pangloss and the Baron! Martin is also amazed. Looking at Pangloss, he asks, "Is that the great philosopher?"

Candide asks the captain to set a price for the two slaves. The captain thinks about it, and says that since Candide is a Christian cur, and these men are obviously important, he will ask fifty thousand sequins apiece. Candide says he will pay the price, and then, forgetting his mission for the moment, tells the captain to take him back to Constantinople. But then he remembers Cunegonde, and asks the captain to go to her. But the captain heard the first command, and headed the ship back to the city.

Candide embraced Pangloss and the Baron, and each was overjoyed at seeing the other. On arriving at Constantinople, Candide found a Jew to whom he sold a diamond worth one hundred thousand sequins for fifty thousand; the Jew swore by Abraham he could pay no more. Candide took the money, and with it liberated Pangloss and the Baron. They then discussed the question of finding Cunegonde. Candide sold more diamonds to two Jews and off they went.

Comment

Candide's spirits rise and fall sharply in this chapter, but they end on a high note, as he once again finds the Baron and Dr. Pangloss. They have not yet told their stories; this will come in the next chapter. Another important note is Candide's reaction to the news that Cunegonde is now an old, ugly, slave. True to the code of chivalry, still alive in the eighteenth century, he vows not to desert her, and to love her always. Still, a part of him wonders as to the wisdom of this course of action.

CHAPTER TWENTY-EIGHT: WHAT HAPPENED TO CANDIDE, CUNEGONDE, PANGLOSS, MARTIN, AND THE REST

This is another of those chapters in which leading characters tell the amazing stories of their activities while away from Candide.

Candide asks the Baron to forgive him for having struck him with a sword. The Baron thinks Candide behaved badly, but forgives him. He will now tell Candide what happened to him after that incident. He was cured by an apothecary (druggist) at the college, and soon after was captured by Spaniards and imprisoned in Buenos Aires. The Baron then asked to be sent to Rome, and this request was granted. He became chaplain for the French Ambassador at Constantinople after a stay in Rome. One evening, while in Constantinople, he went bathing in the nude with a handsome young page. Although the incident might have been innocent enough, it is a crime for a Christian to be found naked with a Moslem, and so he was sent to the galleys. He doesn't seem to have minded this so much, and is more interested in learning of the fate of his sister.

Candide then turn to Pangloss. What has happened to him? It is true that Candide saw the philosopher executed, but he was supposed to have been burned at the stake. Since it was raining things got so wet that the executioners despaired of lighting the fire, and Pangloss was hanged instead. Afterwards, the body was taken to a surgeon for dissection. The surgeon made an incision from the collar bone to the navel. It seems that Pangloss had been hanged by an incompetent, a man who was fine at burning but knew little of hangings. And so, he was not really dead! When the scalpel went into him, he let out a shout. The surgeon thought he had the devil himself on the table, and ran away, hoping to consult with his wife. She asked why he had to pick a heretic to dissect; didn't he realize that the devil was in each of them? She then ran to a priest, whom she hoped would exorcize the devil. Pangloss was shaken by all of this, but was saved at last by a Portuguese barber who sewed him up. He was well enough after two weeks, and the barber found him a job as footman to a Maltese knight who was on his way to Venice. Once there, Pangloss found employment with a Venetian businessman, who took him to Constantinople. It was there that he got into serious trouble. One day he went into a mosque and saw an old priest and a pretty young girl, who was saying her prayers. There was a bunch of flowers between her breasts, and as she prayed, they fell out. Always the gentleman, Pangloss picked them up and replaced them reverently. But he took so long with the job that the priest was angered. Seeing that he was a Christian, he called for help. Pangloss was taken before a judge and sentenced to the galleys for his crime. It was there that he found the Baron, along with five Neopolitan priests and two monks from Corfu; all had had similar adventures. He and the Baron used to argue over which on had been done the greater injustice, and each received twenty lashes a day, "until the sequence of events ordained in this universe brought you to our galley to ransom us."

Now Candide asks the vital question: did all of these misadventures shake Pangloss' belief that everything was for the best in this world? Pangloss answers that he has not changed his mind on the subject. He is a philosopher, and it would not be proper for philosophers to recant, "especially as Leibnitz cannot be wrong; and besides, the pre-established harmony, together with the plenum and the materia subtilis, is the most beautiful thing in the world."

Comment

The Baron's story is of the type we have come to expect in *Candide*. Candide is told that he was taken to the galley for an **episode** with a young man; thus, Voltaire intimates that homosexuality is to be added to the many other crimes of the clergy. Pangloss' story is the more important. In it Voltaire tells us that the Inquisition has become so specialized as the result of "good business" that the functions of execution have been broken down into hanging and burning, and that burners know little of hanging and vice versa. Because of this, Pangloss was saved. Then Voltaire pokes fun once more at doctors. The body was dissected by a doctor-a man of science who was supposed to be above superstition. Yet, when Pangloss moved, the doctor was convinced that the devil was about to emerge. In the end, the philosopher is saved by an ordinary barber, who apparently knew little of medicine, and so could sew up the cut with no difficulty. Then Pangloss tells us of how he became a galley slave. Once again, a woman was the cause of his ruin. His story is transparent enough; we know what happened in the mosque. The priest was no fool. He first ascertained whether Pangloss was a Christian before calling the police. He knew that such a charge against a Moslem might put him in the galleys! After all of this, Pangloss is still the optimist. Nothing can change his mind, since he is a philosopher. In this way, Voltaire disposes of many of the philosophes who, when confronted with the choice between their ideas about reality and their observations, choose the former. These men are not trustworthy observers or thinkers. They have ideas about man, but have either ignored mankind itself or choose to deny what their senses tell them. Voltaire ends with a direct blast at Liebnitz, who is mentioned by name as expected, Pangloss says that Liebnitz (apparently his mentor) cannot be wrong under any circumstances, and so the world must be for the best.

CHAPTER TWENTY-NINE: HOW CANDIDE FOUND CUNEGONDE AND THE OLD WOMAN ONCE MORE

The travellers had many stories to tell one another, and the occupied themselves easily as the ship went to the place where Cunegonde was a servant. When they finally arrived at the Prince's house and saw Cunegonde and the old woman, they were shocked; Cunegonde was old, ugly, and weather beaten. Even Candide was taken back at the sight. But he composed himself quickly. All embraced, and Candide purchased her freedom and that of the old woman.

There was a small farm nearby, and the old woman suggested that the group go there until their fortunes improved. Cunegonde didn't realize how ugly she had become (no one had told her) and she reminded Candide of his promises. Candide did not deny them, and he told the Baron he planned to marry his sister. But the Baron still maintained that Cunegonde could not marry anyone so low; if she did, her children could not enter the ranks of German society. Cunegonde implored her brother to change his mind, but he was firm. Candide was angry. He told the Baron that he was an unspeakable ass. Without his help the Baron would still be a galley slave. Cunegonde was an ugly crone, and yet when he offers to marry her, the Baron has the nerve to object! If he got any angrier, he would kill the Baron. The Baron remains calm; Candide may kill him, but he will never marry Cunegonde.

Comment

This short chapter is part-afterthought, part-preface (for the concluding chapter). The only point worth mentioning is that the Baron, in common with others of his status, has no sense of gratitude or (more important) reality. He doesn't seem to realize that he has nothing and may hope for nothing. As far as he is concerned status is all. A wealthy commoner may not marry an impoverished, ugly noble. Voltaire always criticized the short-sightedness of the nobility, and here we have another example of this criticism.

CHAPTER THIRTY: CONCLUSION

Candide really didn't want to marry Cunegonde, but the Baron's arrogance made him decide to go through with it. Besides, Cunegonde was so insistent that he couldn't very well back down. He consulted Pangloss, Martin, and Cacambo about the situation. Pangloss proved the Baron had no right to interfere; in accord with Imperial law she could wed Candide with her left hand. Martin suggested they throw the Baron into the sea, while Cacambo thought he might be returned to the galley, and then returned to Rome. They said nothing of this to Cunegonde, but accepted Cacambo's proposal. Thus, they had the double pleasure of punishing a Jesuit and a German baron.

One would think that Candide would now enjoy his life, surrounded by friends and married to Cunegonde. But he had been so badly cheated by the Jews that he had little left of his fortune. Cunegonde had become an ugly old crone, and got worse each day. Cacambo worked in the garden and sold vegetables, and cursed his lot each moment. Pangloss was annoyed that he had not become the luminary of a German university. Martin remained convinced that it was a miserable world, and suffered in silence. The three-Candide, Pangloss, and Martin-sometimes discussed metaphysics and morals. From their farm they could see princes going into exile and others coming to take their places; this added fuel to their arguments. All were bored, and one day the old woman was moved to ask what was worse; to have undergone all her misfortunes or to sit on the farm, with nothing to do? This question produced a new discussion. Martin thought man was destined either to suffer from anxiety or boredom. Candide disagreed, but said nothing. Pangloss admitted he had a hard time of it, but still thought all would turn out well. However, he really didn't believe it.

One day Martin's pessimism seemed vindicated, much to the distress of Pangloss and Candide. Pacquette and Brother Giroflee arrived at the farm; they had spent the money Candide had given them, quarreled, separated, then come together once more. They went to prison, and then escaped. Giroflee converted to Islam, while Pacquette returned to her old profession of prostitution. Martin thought this justified his pessimism; none of them was happy. Even Pangloss was distraught.

The companions learned that a famous Turkish philosopher lived nearby, and they went to visit him. Pangloss, their spokesman, asked the philosopher why man was born. The philosopher, a dervish, asked why that was any of Pangloss' business. Candide asked if the philosopher would admit that there was much evil in the world. So what, asked the philosopher? Does Candide think the King worries if mice on a ship are comfortable? (He implies here that God is the King, and he has little concern over the fate of man or his comfort.) Pangloss asks what should be done. The dervish tells him that the best thing to do is keep his mouth shut. Pangloss would not be still; he tells the dervish that he wanted to talk to him about "cause and effect, the best of all possible worlds, the origin of evil, the nature of the soul, and pre-established harmony." With this, the dervish slams the door in his face.

During the time they were with the dervish, some cabinet ministers in Constantinople where strangled and their friends impaled. This created a stir of conversation. On their way back to the farm, the companions noticed an old man sitting at his door, on a nearby farm. Pangloss asked the old man whether he knew the name of one of the deceased, a judge. The old man confessed he was ignorant of such things, but knew that those who entered politics came to a bad end and deserved it. He doesn't bother about such things; his goods are sent to Constantinople, and that's enough for him. The old man then invited the companions into his home. They ate, and the old man's daughters perfumed their beards. Candide thought the old man had a magnificent estate. The old man said he had only twenty acres, but found that work helps banish boredom, vice, and poverty.

Candide thought of the old man's words as they returned to their farm. He thought the old man had done better for himself than the six kings they had met in Venice. Pangloss had an answer: high position always brings dangers. He then lists many rulers who have suffered. "I also know," says Candide, "that we must go and work in the garden." Pangloss agrees; man was placed in the Garden of Eden in order to make it better. This proves that man was not meant for an easy life. Martin thinks that work without argument is the only way to make life bearable.

Everyone agreed to that statement, and set about implementing it. The estate was small, but it prospered. Cunegonde was ugly, but she made excellent pastry. Pacquette proved clever at embroidery, and the old woman took care of the linen. All worked, even Brother Giroflee. And from time to time,

Pangloss would say to Candide: "There is a chain of events in this best of all possible worlds; for if you had not been turned out of the beautiful castle for love of Lady Cunegonde, and if you had not been involved in the Inquisition, and had not wandered over America on foot, and had not struck the Baron with your sword, and lost all those sheep you brought from Eldorado, you would not be here eating candied fruit and pistachio nuts." Candide agrees, but adds that "we must go and work in the garden."

Comment

This is probably the most important chapter in *Candide*. Here Voltaire sums up, and presents his answers for the world's ills. His companions all have troubles, and go to see the famous dervish. All this gentleman can tell them is to live and shut up. He is impatient with Pangloss, and will not discuss those great problems which Pangloss, has spent his life analyzing; to him they are worthless. There is no plan in the universe; only chaos. God exists, but he does not worry about the individual human, who must learn to care for himself. Then the companions see the old man. He lives on his small farm, works hard, does not concern himself with the outside world, and seems happy. Hard work and minding one's own business is his answer for the world's problems. With this, Candide and his friends return to their farm, and try the old man's formula. It seems to work. Only Pangloss clings to the old philosophy; all has turned out for the best precisely because of all their difficulties. Candide's answer to this statement is most interesting. This may be true, he says, but we have to work in the garden. Does Voltaire mean to say that the best course for mankind is minding its own business? Is he denying the importance of philosophy?. Does he find that the world's ills can be cured by a return to the soil? Does he imply that Candide has turned his back on the Pangloss creed? All of these questions remain unanswered.

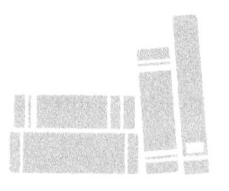

CANDIDE

CHARACTER ANALYSIS

As has been mentioned, *Candide* is an allegory of the human condition as seen by Voltaire. The novel was not written to amuse, and we are not supposed to "identify" with the hero in the usual sense of the term. Today most novels are viewed as allegories, and most of them attempt to be as subtle as possible. The tradition of the eighteenth century was quite different. *Everyman* and *Pilgrim's Progress* were part of the heritage of the people of this century. These were broad, obvious allegories, in the style readers were accustomed to in the period. It was natural, then, that Voltaire would write in this tradition, making the characters in *Candide* easily identifiable by observing this context. This method of presenting ideas is not unusual today, nor was it unusual in the eighteenth century. Samuel Johnson's *Rasselas,* which has been compared with *Candide* both in style, approach, and story, was written at about the same time as Voltaire's work.

The leading characters in *Candide* are analyzed in the following pages. They are discussed in order of their relative importance to the story. Note that Pangloss is discussed immediately after *Candide*. Although he is absent for most of the book, his influence on the hero is visible throughout.

Candide

The name Candide is derived from the Latin, candidus, which means white, and usually symbolized innocence in ancient writings. It also means candid, and our hero is nothing if not that. He looks at the world and tells us exactly what he sees (as influenced by the teachings of Pangloss).

Pangloss

The name of Candide's teacher is derived from the Greek pan and glossa, which means all languages. In the vernacular of the time, this meant "windbag." The philosopher was modeled after Liebnitz, Pope, Shaftesbury, and other optimistic thinkers of the period. The reader must remember that *Candide* is a purposeful **satire**; Voltaire realized that his opponents did not hold the ridiculous ideas he ascribes to Pangloss. Rather, the author attempts to show what these ideas could become if carried to their logical conclusions.

Martin

Candide's companion joins him at a time when he is ready to denounce Pangloss' optimism. Just as the philosopher argued that all is for the best, so Martin thought all was for the worst. In other words, he is the other side of the coin, as gloomy as Pangloss is cheerful. Voltaire is more sympathetic toward Martin than he is toward Pangloss, but the reader must remember that *Candide* was written to attack the optimists, and not the pessimists, this job is taken care of in other writings. In this respect, the reader should recall that Candide rejects both men in the last chapter of the book.

Cacambo

Candide's guide in the New World was probably given his name by Voltaire because it resembled cacao and other words which suggested America to the European reader of the eighteenth century. There is also a scatological **connotation** to the name which we need not go into here. It implies, among other things, a half-breed origin. Cacambo then is a wily American half-breed. He stands in perfect juxtaposition to the Baron, who has a fine lineage, but whose character is as black as Cacambo's is pure. Some have seen in Cacambo the prefiguration of roughish characters found in later works. For example, he resembles Figaro, a major character in later Italian tales and operas. Some have seen in Cacambo a copy of Sancho Panza, Don Quixote's companion, but this seems rather overdrawn.

Cunegonde

This is also a name which was chosen for sound as well as meaning. The alliterative effect of Candide and Cunegonde is perfect (some say Voltaire chose Cacambo for the same reason). Cunegonde is an old name, and there were several queens by that name in medieval history. Like the name Cacambo, there is a scatological **connotation** which may have pleased Voltaire as well, since he was fond of such things. Cunegonde represents many things: chivalric love at one point, hard-headed **realism** at another. Too, there are really several Cunegondes: the one seen by Candide is pure and virtuous; the version we receive is a beautiful, shrewd wench who knows her way around. She is one of the few characters in the book who develops: in the beginning, she is an innocent young girl; in the end, she is a wise woman of the world. At first, she is coquettish with Candide; in the end, she demands he marry her.

The Old Woman

Here is a classic type in French fiction, an old maid who is full of sound advice. We meet her early in the book when she serves as Cunegonde's maid. Later on, Cunegonde turns into a perfect double of the old woman. Abigail also serves as a counterpart to Cacambo, and echoes many of his ideas in a feminine voice. Voltaire uses her at times to voice his reflections on the state of the world.

Pacquette

The name of the serving-girl, turned prostitute, means daisy, a sweet name for an innocent girl whose misfortunes parallel in many ways those of her mistress, Cunegonde, and those of the old woman. One suspects that Pacquette, like Cunegonde, will wind up being like the old woman.

Pococurante

This name means caring little. He is the jaded man of the world, who has seen all and enjoyed all. He has found that nothing is satisfying, and is bored. Some of his comments on the thinkers of the past reflect the judgements of Voltaire, but the reader must not think that Voltaire has made Pococurante an admirable figure. He is what Candide would have become had he no difficulties in life. Voltaire tells us, through the words of Martin, that there is pleasure in not being pleased; Pococurante has never known this pleasure. In some ways, the two men go together well. Martin tells us that all is for the worst; Pococurante shows us that even the best is for the worst.

Brother Giroflee

The name means wallflower. Voltaire may have used it because it goes well with his companion, Pacquette (daisy). One scholar has noted that it may also be interpreted as a slap which leaves a mark on the face, and certainly Giroflee's life was ample testimony for the choice of the name if this interpretation is accepted. He is introduced into the story to help carry it along, and also as a symbol of the stupidity of such feudal institutions as primogeniture and the nature of vocations in the Church.

Baron Thunder-ten-tronckh

The name of the barony was chosen for sound more than anything else. It is a perfect reflection of the pomposity and pettiness of the small baronies of that part of Europe. As for the Baron, he appears in many guises in the story. One may assume his father's character is his as well: that of a vain, blustering tyrant. Then the son is a warrior-saint of the Jesuits, killing with abandon, with no vocation, enjoying his life in Paraguay. Finally, he appears as a down-at-the-heels aristocrat, now a homosexual. At all times he is arrogant and narrow-sighted. Even while a galley-slave he cannot forget his ancestors. When Candide offers to marry his sister, he refuses to consent. As badly-wrecked as she might be, she is still of noble birth, and cannot marry Candide. To Voltaire, the Baron represents the nobility of Europe which, as another writer put it, "has learned nothing and forgotten nothing." This characteristic will eventually lead to the destruction of the class; in *Candide,* it leads to the Baron's destruction.

CANDIDE

ESSAY QUESTIONS AND ANSWERS

Question: Carl Becker discusses the role of "the Heavenly City" in his work on the Enlightenment. What was Voltaire's thought on such places? How did the vision of utopia manifest itself in *Candide?*

Answer: The reader must remember that Voltaire lived in a sort of heavenly city; his home in Switzerland, a garden similar in some respects to the one *Candide* finally found outside of Constantinople. He was quite content there, and yet he ventured from the place, and in the end died in Paris, and not his beloved home.

The utopian societies discussed in *Candide* are of a different order. There are five in number. Three of them, all agrarian and patterned in part after statements and ideas of Rousseau, are found in America. These are: the land of the Oreillons, the Jesuit kingdom in Paraguay, and Eldorado. Two are found in Europe: Thunder-ten-tronckh and Constantinople.

The American utopias all have faults. The Oreillons, patterned after Rousseau's *Noble Savages*, live in a state of nature. Voltaire does not mention their government or laws, and we are led to assume they have nothing but a primitive tribal arrangement. Rousseau intimated and at times said outright that such societies, with all property in common possession, would show none of the anti-social manifestations so common in Europe. Voltaire disagrees: the Oreillons are cannibals, considering Jesuits a prime delicacy. Cacambo explains that this is not really barbaric, and thinks the Europeans would do the same had they not better food. Similarly, he defends the cohabitation of Oreillon girls with monkeys on the grounds that Candide does not understand that this is not a European society, and must be allowed its own peculiarities. Still, these defenses are not convincing. Voltaire, in using them, is probably ridiculing those who defend differences in cultures on such grounds. And so, he dismisses the Oreillon utopia by having his hero leave there as soon as he can, after being saved by telling the Indians that he has killed Jesuits.

The Jesuit Kingdom, a theocracy similar in some ways to the Geneva of Calvin which Voltaire knew well, is also flawed. The Baron lives well; all he wishes is at his disposal. But Voltaire makes us aware of the continual presence of Jesuit-soldiers. Without them, the oppressed Indians would surely rise and overthrow their rulers. Thus, this type of utopia is maintained by fear of an upper class which enjoys life, but has no end other than continual expansion. Candide flees this land as soon as he can.

Then our hero goes to Eldorado. Here all seems well; people live long, healthy lives, are free from want, and use reason in all things. This is indeed the heavenly city described by many philosophes. But even here there are problems. No one works; all is free and plentiful. Without work, can man find meaning in life? Voltaire thinks not. In addition, the author asks if the life of reason is what man wants and needs. Again, he answers in the negative. After loading the sheep with gold and precious stones, Candide and Cacambo flee this earthly paradise.

What, then, of the European utopias? Thunder-ten-tronckh is an idyllic place, in some ways resembling the Jesuit lands in Paraguay. It is no accident that the Baron's father is comfortable and happy in Thunder-ten-tronckh, and his son finds joy in Paraguay. But like the American kingdom, the European barony is fine for the upper classes, but misery for all others.

Constantinople-or to be more precise, Candide's farm outside of Constantinople-is about as perfect a place that man can hope to find. Candide works in his garden, and seems to have found happiness. Note that such a farm was within the grasp of many philosophes; Voltaire himself lived on one. And yet, it is irrational, contains many of the flaws of Europe, and does not correct the inconsistencies of human nature. What, then makes it a near-perfect utopia? Voltaire indicates that work is the universal solvent of human despair. When Pangloss attempts to justify the events of Candide's life, our hero almost ignores him. The best of all possible worlds for him is a place where each tends his own garden. There, one can mind his own business, and most important, have business to mind. The active life, separated in part from the maddening crowd and the stupidities of European society, are the answers for Voltaire. Yet, he is not an anti-intellectual, as is Rousseau. His garden is one of reason, and not of emotion and irrationalism.

Question: What is the "message" and "philosophy" of *Candide?*

Answer: Allegories usually have messages-the hero of Pilgrims' Progress finds his goal in God. What is the message and philosophy of *Candide?* Is it merely "We must go and work in the garden?" This is part of the answer: man finds contentment in meaningful occupations. But it is by no means all of the answer, or even most of it. It leaves many questions unanswered. For example, what is Voltaire's attitude toward optimism? Toward pessimism? Is the correct stance that of the skeptics? The cynics? There are no satisfactory answers to these questions, because Voltaire was unable to find them in his own life.

The author spent his life attacking the shibboleths of eighteenth century society. Wherever he looked he saw irrational, sometimes cruel, and useless institutions. Among these he numbered the Church, the State, war, unjust laws, and almost everything else that touched man, including philosophy itself and love. Having "swept the philosophical stables clean" he was at a loss as to what to replace these institutions with. In the end, Voltaire became an epicurean, viewing life as an accident, which was to be enjoyed while alive. But is this a satisfactory answer? Is there nothing better for mankind than enjoyment and work? Although Voltaire never says so directly, he seems to imply as much in his writings, including *Candide*.

How did Voltaire arrive at this conclusion? One might note that there are only three ways to meet an unsatisfactory situation. One may resign oneself to it, the conditions may be fought, or the individual may leave his society. Voltaire considered all of these possibilities. As for the last, leaving the stupidities of Europe was no answer; there are stupidities everywhere, although each society produces its own version. As we have seen, the utopias of America are no more satisfactory to *Candide* than the problems of Europe. Can one leave his milieu mentally through the transports of love? Such departures do not last, as witnessed by Candides falling out of love with Cunegonde, the object of his search for almost the entire book.

What of resignation? This is not the answer either, for it leads to a sterile, empty life, a devoid of meaning. In addition, is it possible to resign oneself to conditions? One of the messages to be found in *Candide* is that life consists of the continual facing up to challenges. Without these, life is meaningless. It was the lack of abrasive conflict, and not so much the lack of Cunegonde, that sent Candide from the state of Eldorado.

The remaining alternative, that of struggle, is the one accepted by Voltaire, and also by *Candide*. One must attempt to correct individual ills, realizing all the time that a complete transformation of society and man is not only impossible, but perhaps undesirable as well. In the end Candide comes to terms with society; he does not attempt to make society over in his own image.

Question: What were the immediate and long-range implications of Voltaire's works and philosophy?

Answer: Voltaire lived at the center of intellectual life during the eighteenth century; it is impossible to think of the Enlightenment without mentioning his name. But what of the implications of his ideas? Voltaire's passion for reform and hatred of irrational forces in French life had many political and social implications. The expulsion of the Jesuits from France was an indirect result of his teachings. The attempts on the parts of Turgot and Necker to reform France's finances were inspired (we have Turgot's word for this) by Voltaire's writings. Indeed, the first stage of the French Revolution was traced by many of the participants to Voltaire.

The French Revolution may be considered the great endowment of Voltaire's philosophy and life-and its failure as well. The France of 1789 was controlled by the heirs of Baron Thunder-ten-tronckh. These men had political and social powers, without a knowledge of society or politics, intelligence, or compassion. France was not the most irrational nation in Europe in this regard, but the accumulated institutions of a thousand years did not make sense to the men of the French Enlightenment-the philosophes-and their middle-class allies. At first they attempted to reform French life. They met strong opposition from the nobles, the King, and the Church, but they pressed on, and accomplished many of their goals. But it was here that their mechanistic philosophy failed them. They had assumed that once shown reason, man would create reasonable institutions. This was not to be in France, for the revolution gathered steam and entered its irrational, bloody stage. Even then, while under the control of men like Robespierre, attempts were made to reconstruct life through the use of models created by the philosophes. Again, these attempts met with failures, and finally ended in the despotism of Napoleon, and a return to the old regime after the Emperor's defeat.

The course of the French Revolution illustrates the successes- and failures-of Voltaire and the philosophes. These men spent much time in criticizing existing institutions, but not enough in formulating workable alternatives. This failure is vividly seen in *Candide*. In it, Voltaire attempts to pull down almost every institution in France-including the philosophes themselves. But when it comes time for him to present his alternative, he has no better solution than work and isolation. Voltaire's works were calculated to lead to action, but the philosopher was not sure himself what the results of the action should be. It was his misfortune to speak radically, but think conservatively. He opposed the Church, but admitted that man was immoral, and needed restraints. He lampooned the State, but did not think that man in a state of nature could perform well. Voltaire decried medicine, but maintained himself near the finest doctors in Europe. In other words-to paraphrase Pangloss and Martin-this is the worst of worlds, but not the worst possible. Voltaire called for reforms, but at times indicated that reform might be worse than the evil it replaced.

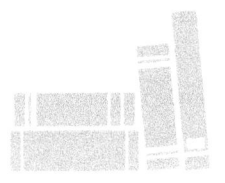

CANDIDE

ANNOTATED BIBLIOGRAPHY

Cabeen, David C., ed. *A Critical Bibliography of French Literature*. George Havens and Donald Bond have written an excellent summary of eighteenth century French thought for this large collection. Included is a good short study of Voltaire and his philosophy, a bibliography of works on *Candide* and other selections by Voltaire, as well as an analysis of the book.

Cobban, Alfred. *In Search of Humanity*. A good short discussion of the Enlightenment, including deft analyses of the major thinkers of the period, their successes and failures. Cobban has a chapter on "Voltaire and the War on Religion" and another on "Idealism and Pessimism" that are well-worth reading before going into *Candide*.

Frame, Donald, ed. *Voltaire's Candide, Zadig, and Selected Stories*. A handy, easily available collection of some of Voltaire's shorter works, including *Candide*. Frame's sort introduction contains the highlights of Voltaire's life.

Brandes, Georg. *Voltaire*. A massive work, originally published in two volumes, which is one of the most complete and best studies of the author. Brandes tends to ramble at times, and go off into unproductive tangents. His material on the relations between Voltaire and other Enlightenment thinkers is quite good.

Durant, Will and Ariel. *The Age of Voltaire*. This is another volume in the huge, important, and influential history of civilization which has been in the writing for more than forty years. The Durants write well, show many insights, and are thoroughly enjoyable. Although this book, like others in the series, contains little original material, it is perhaps the best single source for the novice who wishes to study the Enlightenment.

Wade, Ira. *Voltaire and Candide*. If you can "wade through Wade," you will find this book illuminating and enjoyable. Unfortunately, the author has written primarily for scholars who have a knowledge of French. This volume contains a complete copy of the first edition of *Candide* as part of the appendix.

Bottiglia, William. *Voltaire's Candide: Analysis of A Classic*. This is Volume VII in the series, "Studies on Voltaire and the Eighteenth Century." It is dedicated to Wade, and smacks of his pedantry. In other words, it is a fine study for the expert, but should be approached by the novice with some care. Bottiglia has written what amounts to a compendium of the thoughts of others as well as his own interesting insights. It is well worth reading, and the student should not let the scholarly paraphernalia scare him unduly.

Aldington, Richard. *Voltaire*. An old but still useful biography. Aldington is preferable to Brandes in many respects. It is shorter, more readable, and contains a good analysis of Voltaire's weaknesses as a writer and thinker.

Becker, Carl. *The Heavenly City of the Eighteenth Century Philosophers*. This is a classic, and should not be missed. Becker stresses the continuity of thought from the Middle Ages to the Enlightenment, and the role of faith, rather than reason, during the eighteenth century. Voltaire emerges as a high priest of reason, and not as the skeptic so many others think him to be.

Barber, William. *Leibnitz in France, from Arnauld to Voltaire*. This is an essential work for students who wish to better understand Voltaire's opposition to the optimistic creeds of the period.

Carr, Herbert. *Leibnitz*. A short work on the German philosopher and his followers. Carr has written a section on the background to *Candide* from the point of view of the Leibnitz group, which will give the reader a better-balanced view of the period and the man.

Gay, Peter. *Voltaire's Politics*. Gay is a leading scholar of the period. In this work, he discusses the impact of Voltaire's ideas on the many reform movements of the period, which were a backdrop to the French Revolution.

Havens, George. *Age of Ideas*. This is an excellent analysis of the Enlightenment by a man who has spent his life in the study. Havens has a section on *Candide* which is essential for any student of the book. The reader is further encouraged to read other works by Havens, who is probably the most influential Voltaire scholar.

Josephson, Matthew. *Jean-Jacques Rousseau*. Josephson is an American writer of popular histories with a left-wing bias. He favors *Rausseau*, and includes in his biography an interesting discussion of the conflicts and friendships between his subject and other philosophers of the period, including Voltaire.

Lewis, Joseph. *Voltaire, the Incomparable Infidel*. Lewis is a leading American atheist, whose praise for Voltaire knows no bounds. This book is interesting from this viewpoint, but contains little which is not to be found in other, better works.

Maurois, Andre. *Voltaire*. A readable life of Voltaire which is interesting, and at times exciting.

Meyer, Adolph. *Voltaire: Man of Justice*. The author is unrestrained in his praise of Voltaire. This book is valuable for Meyer's discussion of the reactions to *Candide* by contemporaries.

Shilling, Bernard. *Conservative England and the Case Against Voltaire.* Voltaire admired English freedoms, but many of those who were responsible for these freedoms (and those who opposed him) thought Voltaire to be a dangerous radical, especially in regard to his writings on religion. This opposition is fully discussed in Shilling's excellent book.

Torrey, Norman. *Voltaire and the English Deists.* While accepting some of Shilling's material and conclusions, Torrey believes that English writers had a great impact on Voltaire, who understood that nation better than Shilling believes he did.

EXPLORE THE ENTIRE LIBRARY OF BRIGHT NOTES STUDY GUIDES

From Shakespeare to Sinclair Lewis and from Plato to Pearl S. Buck, The Bright Notes Study Guide library spans hundreds of volumes, providing clear and comprehensive insights into the world's greatest literature. Discover more, faster with the Bright Notes Study Guide to the classics you're reading today.

STUDY GUIDE TO GREAT EXPECTATIONS BY CHARLES DICKENS

STUDY GUIDE TO THE ROMANTIC POETS BY PETRONIUS

STUDY GUIDE TO BELOVED BY TONI MORRISON

STUDY GUIDE TO ROMEO AND JULIET BY WILLIAM SHAKESPEARE

STUDY GUIDE TO WUTHERING HEIGHTS BY EMILY BRONTË

See the entire library of available Bright Notes guides at **BrightNotes.com**

Available in print and digital wherever books are sold

IP INFLUENCE PUBLISHERS